RETHINKING
HUMAN
CAPITAL

From Job to GIG — A Competency-Based Tool

RETHINKING
HUMAN
CAPITAL

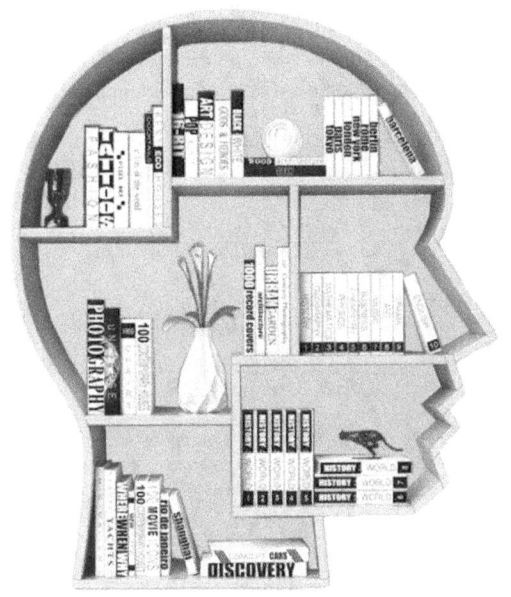

STEFANIA DINKLAGE
PATRICK O. CONNELLY & BRAD MUELLER

Copyrighted Material

Rethinking Human Capital: From Job to GIG

Copyright © 2021 by Commercial Insights LLC.
All Rights Reserved.

No part of this publication may be reproduced, stored
in a retrieval system or transmitted, in any form or by any
means—electronic, mechanical, photocopying, recording or
otherwise—without prior written permission from the publisher,
except for the inclusion of brief quotations in a review.

For information about this title or to order other books
and/or electronic media, contact the publisher:

Stefania Dinklage
stefanie@commercialinsights.ch

Patrick O. Connelly
Brad Mueller
www.commercialinsights.ch
info@commercialinsights.ch

Printed in the United States of America

Cover design: Laura Dinklage
Interior design: 1106 Design

Table of Contents

Preface vii

Authors in Brief xiii

Acknowledgment xv

Introduction xvii

Chapter I 1
 Innovative concept—Competency

Chapter II 23
 The Historical Pattern That Led to the Current Dilemma

Chapter III 41
 Current Model for Securing Human Resources

Chapter IV 65
 Rethinking a Pattern of Behavior

Chapter V 125
 Given the Status Quo—a Quantum Leap

Chapter VI 143
   A Context for Optimizing a Scalable Human Resource Pool

Epilogue 175
   The Journey Continues

Appendix I 187
   Institutional Support for the Unemployed

Appendix II 217

Appendix III 219

Appendix IV 221

Appendix V 223

Glossary 227

References 233

Index 237

Preface

This book represents the work product and result of several years of research and experience into the methodology and effectiveness of human resource management—how resources are attracted, selected, retained, and developed in order to optimize value both to the individuals and to markets. The authors contribute an interesting amalgam of education and experience as well as a unique understanding of the factors that now lead to the presentation of the Competency Paradigm.

Together, the authors bring nearly a century of experience in education, psychology, and business among diverse global markets and cultures to bear on an increasingly more difficult challenge . . . the optimization of resources both internal and external with a goal of establishing a **twitch-agile**[1] entity within an economically efficient framework.

Having directly experienced the results of an inefficient system of resource selection over the last few decades in many different industries and markets, the team has concentrated

---

[1] A condition wherein an enterprise reacts quickly to business challenges utilizing its resources most effectively.

expertise in aspects of business performance that addresses the move toward a more responsive, agile, and efficient model. This book represents a move toward taking full advantage of the value of the method to be presented in this book. Talent and human resource managers must advance from a job-descriptive, resume-intensive search-and-secure structure to a competency-based search that optimizes the true value of both individual and pooled resources.

Further, the search can be executed both within and beyond the enterprise to enable current needs-analysis response and medium- and even long-term strategic planning.

Alternatively, failure to adapt organizations to this 21st-century strategy—which promotes more rapid adaptation, functional agility, and challenge response—lowers an enterprise's competitive advantage and sustains typical silo thinking that restricts growth. In the end, the process is self-defeating.

The leadership team consists of three seasoned executives, each with specific knowledge and experience, forming an integral pool of competencies that has proven successful in the implementation of various projects around the world.

A dialogue among these experts assessed and then analyzed the potential of such a major shift from job-descriptive hiring practices to competency-assessment and -fulfillment practices. They provide a unique perspective on the diverse challenges faced by modern organizations. This book was co-authored by a team with a history of successful insolvency and business turnaround, talent management, and, in general, helping organizations in need of an alternate strategy to improve and indeed optimize the resources of the enterprise.

An observation that prevails from past initiatives is that many organizational structures focus on narrow fixed and semi-fixed "silo" functionality, position-centered and skill-level targeted. The results lead toward an inherently less-agile response to market conditions, impairing effective team execution and retarding a more holistic and professional development of resident skills and an awareness of the real potential of enterprise talent.

Perhaps the greatest opportunity presented by the concepts in this book resides in a better understanding of the actual bounds of internal/external competency across diverse areas of expertise and the availability to the enterprise. This book articulates the alternative view and suggests a methodology to restructure business processes into competencies and, further, to standardize them into a common vocabulary and framework.

Amidst an economic and medical crisis unparalleled in recent history, this book introduces a process that represents a major paradigm shift. Human resource management is deconstructed into a skill, knowledge, and experience construct to identify key elements that lead to the identification and selection of talent that fulfills the needs of a competitive enterprise. The myriad of dimensions through which the authors approach human resource management represents a departure from the traditional applicant-assessment techniques, replacing these with an approach that identifies both resident competencies and required additional competencies to create an optimal solution to fulfill an enterprise's current and future needs.

Further, the paradigm stimulates interest in understanding that the recognition of gaps in desirable competencies is as important as competency affirmation in the creation of a strategic-development plan—the former important to the strategic solution of the current business plan, and the latter critical to the forward-looking strategy of the enterprise. This represents a major shift in traditional human resource management and one that the authors believe will represent a quantum leap forward in the overall economic efficiency of the enterprise.

Implementation will also require a change in methodology and the traditional thinking used to define a successful candidate or associate. The authors instead focus on the incremental talents, the competencies, and the sub-competencies that combine to present the suitable candidate—internal resident or external, perhaps GIG[2]—associate required to satisfy enterprise needs.

---

[2] An event characterized by a commitment of resource to a specific temporary requirement of time and effort.

Internally, HR organizations must demonstrate an ability to select, train, and more fully, if not completely, utilize all competencies in the talent pool effectively within a context of rapid change. The challenge will force organizations to rapidly configure and reconfigure solutions using all available internal and external talent resources in order to meet challenges. The process essentially establishes both an internal and external "GIG marketplace," thus integrating competencies from an extended resource pool.

The book presents a value proposition further promoting continuous improvement, learning, and bridging gaps in desirable and necessary competencies, integrating and combining the best features among trade/vocational, academic training, and professional business experience. This formidable model integrates a much broader spectrum of knowledge and makes many more resources available, in a much more efficient manner and with a more interesting cost structure, to interested parties.

In order to establish this value, it is necessary to abandon the narrow focus of the past on job titles and descriptions and realign focus upon the identification and development of a wider array of competencies, the aggregate that may be brought to bear upon challenges faster and more efficiently in response to modern market demands.

Given current global market challenges that may not resolve themselves in the near future, the competency framework this work presents provides an economically efficient solution. The standardized and scalable nature of the model enables a flexibility that supports continuous improvement of the base and as a consequence a growing capability to respond to challenges in a timely manner. The nature of the model is almost heuristic, adjusting content to introduce improvement, identify opportunities, and promote enterprise growth accordingly.

The idea for the book evolved from discussions both internal and external, among executives bemoaning the fact that extremely talented resources were being lost as organizations responded to fiscal pressures in standard ways. Decisions were being made according to position; those viewed as dispensable were the first to be severed, regardless of the body of knowledge represented by the individual position-holder.

Our team debated for several months over the creation of a rationale that supported a continuity of the archaic process... and failed to establish a reasonable argument to continue this process. The work product in this book presents an alternative solution to the status quo and delivers a methodology to characterize, classify, recognize, utilize, and optimize enterprise resources previously unknown or, at the least, underutilized. This solution is at once impactful to both top and bottom lines of enterprises and worthy of consideration. That is why you find yourself here.

Authors in Brief

Stefanie Dinklage: A diverse career extending over more than two decades that includes significant expertise ranging across seven languages combined with success in both academic and business environments. Early concentration in the hospitality industry provided insight into leadership, management, and human resource development, and led to an advanced degree in Business and Behavioral Psychology. Consulting and training in the shared-service industry presented a unique consulting opportunity to delve into the functionality of the complete business cycle, more specifically, the critical order-to-cash cycle. That experience introduced targeted and deeper insight into the selection and development of the key resources necessary to the success of both public and private enterprises throughout Europe. The aggregate of these experiences resulted in a kernel that became the topic of a number of published articles promoting the rethinking of methodologies used to assess talent and talent management. The essence is captured in this book and provides guidance toward a common competency framework and the more practically and economically efficient utilization of human resources.

Brad Mueller: Global leader experienced in turnarounds, business startups, mergers, acquisitions, divestments, and selling businesses for profit. He has diverse, international experience in marketing, sales, operations, engineering, finance, and information systems in the consumer-products, nuclear, office-supply, lamination and plastics, capital-equipment, packaging, software, security, scientific-instrumentation, and X-ray industries. Sixteen years proven P & L results. Designed, built, staffed, and started up three businesses in the US and Korea. Negotiated joint ventures, customer contracts and large-supplier agreements. Entrepreneurial executive with a proven track record in recruiting, training, and developing self-directed work teams.

Prof. Patrick O. Connelly: Career global trade and risk management manufacturing-and-distribution executive and university undergraduate and graduate professor for the last forty years. Expertise extends to developing successful business processes in challenging markets such as the People's Republic of China, South East Asia, as well as European and Latin American market sectors. Publications include dozens of professional articles and authorship of three editions of *Trade Credit Risk Management: Fundamentals of the Craft in Theory and Practice*, supporting global professional certification in credit risk management.

Acknowledgment

As *with all book projects*, it is important to highlight key support extended to us by others that, in the end, contributed to the completed work and resulted in an event of publication and, hopefully, success. As lead author, I acknowledge the influence of both co-authors Patrick O. Connelly and Brad Mueller for sharing countless hours of discussion and debate that enabled the formulation of the idea that became this book.

To colleagues and friends at Alexion, my thanks for expanding the experience brought to bear with their unique and important insights that individually and collectively enabled a broader base upon which to apply their perspective and test the reality of competency-based management.

Personally, I owe special thanks to my soul mates Carl Silva and Ann-May Baur Barat for enabling the conversion of my thoughts into functioning technological results, no small task, indeed. To my daughters Laura and Katharina, whose support and patience were instrumental to my success, my love, my thanks, and my hopes that the paradigm introduced in the book may return their investment in me in a more tangible way for their careers.

Finally, as a team, we would like to acknowledge the efforts of myriad acquaintances, editors, and the publisher for supporting the production of this book.

INTRODUCTION

As *the reader moves through this book*, he is reminded that a common vocabulary is the foundation of today's business world. We are accustomed to definitions of basic concepts, as well as "business," "employee," "job," "position," "title," "job description," "organizational chart," "competency," "level of performance," and, of course, "hierarchical structure" found primarily in more structured organizations. All of which served to facilitate the challenge of understanding the aspects of the business that enable productive and profitable growth.

EVOLVING THE BUSINESS

How did the business life begin? How did mankind arrive at these terms? What actual meaning was given to these terms? More importantly, what has mankind assigned to these terms over the millennia? How were these terms used on a daily basis, and how were they introduced into our lives? This book covers the history of "business" with its terms from three dimensions—The Past, The Present and The Future.

We will give examples from the Middle Ages, such as the shoemaker, who started out making a pair of shoes, and then grew his one-man shop into a family business, creating his own business model and talent pool. This often resulted later in specializations of talent to introduce a higher level of expertise that allowed the store to attract a more desirable clientele.

We will also see that one of the most important and critical production factors for a company is its employee pool. Proper and diligent implementation and promotion of an onboarding process that ensures effective selection, regulation, development, and optimization of resources is an essential component of business success.

In this modern age, it is no longer acceptable or economically efficient to employ factors that do not perform up to the level of their potential. New equipment is introduced that is more efficient, requires less energy and maintenance, and produces output at multiples of predecessor machines. Similarly, in an Information Age, human resources now represent opportunities to improve the actual economic value of each hire both initially and as they demonstrate a contribution to the growth of the business.

Creating an environment that selects talent, establishes previously untapped resources within the employee, and directs that value toward areas of specific importance to the business results in an accelerated organic and profitable growth. Further, it encourages loyalty by stimulating motivated employees to recognize and be recognized for the contribution.

The control or management requirements of growth benefit from a more stable, loyal, and accountable population of employees, managers, and leaders that, as a result of their improved [productive] longevity, can convey a more stable business more competitively across sometimes volatile markets. Clearly, this represents a win-win condition.

Human resources or factors of production, in order to best benefit the business, require both a willingness to produce and an environment that effectively utilizes talents both recognized and unrecognized that contribute to the level of satisfaction [desirably delight] in which they hold the relationship with the business. Past experiences have demonstrated that merely conveying a sense of some level of previous capability and a willingness to take on the challenge as described in a particular job description was sufficient to support the hiring of a resource. Is there any wonder why turnover, both intended and unintended, rose so egregiously over the past century?

Challenged markets and production targets under stress have forced business to stretch its understanding of productivity to include a review of the human resource factor in order to introduce more and better utility and output from this value.

Extracting more value from a given resource, especially the complicated human resource, requires a look at production and satisfaction from both viewpoints: employer and employee. The business seeks a capability to execute tasks in such a way as to produce an output in an acceptable time frame at an acceptable cost. This is all well and good in a static environment, where the process is stable, and there is little variable change. This is clearly not the case with trade, local or global.

Further, tasks have been relegated to silos described in fixed ways as enumerated in job descriptions, with acceptable behavior confined to achieving targets tied to narrow administrative objectives. I refer the reader to any job description for guidance. The rote execution of historical process often adequately serves the immediate needs of the hiring business: producing customer sales, billing expeditiously, converting invoices to cash, etc.

However, enterprise economic growth and competitive advantage require a new mindset in order to optimize value and promote success. The truly effective enterprise will be the one that extracts the *full value* of *competencies* resident within, or to be selected by, the enterprise. In short, we have become prisoners of the past and our past thinking regarding people and their ability to add value to the enterprise.

Business has evolved mostly along technological lines. The application of these technologies drove the new products or services offered to the marketplace. The evolution of the human element has always taken a back seat, evolving slowly over time until the human stresses became too great, and large changes occurred in rapid succession, as in the periodic labor strife.

It is important to take a step back and review how we arrived at this point in time so that we may contemplate properly the future. The paradigm proposed by this book is intended to shake that archaic thinking to its roots.

Chapter 1

INNOVATIVE CONCEPT—COMPETENCY

A *rising buzzword in the current business* vocabulary is the term "competency." Historically simple to define, it represents a condition wherein an individual has demonstrated advanced skill and knowledge representative of a high-level command of the desired behavior. However, the concept of competency is often confused with the elements that, in aggregate, result in the achievement of competency. So how better to understand competency? Whence is the term derived? Why does it now become important to competitive advantage in markets?

The term and concept date back to the late 18th century and refer to the act of striving ". . . in common or after something independently, in company with or together," with others. In its original form, the term related to the act of acquiring certain elements of knowledge, skill, and experience in order to work toward a specific expertise among those characteristics. Classically, the Romans defined it as an action "to meet or come together; agree or coincide;

to be qualified," from *com* ("with," "together" [see *com-*]) + *petere* ("to strive, seek, fall upon, rush at, attack").[3] It may have been more commonly described and defined as presenting a "sufficiency of qualification."

In the sense proposed by this book, "competency" may best be described as a combination of attributes, skills, knowledge, and experience both behavioral and operational, that collectively manifest the potential to bring a high capability to bear in the execution of an expected outcome: simply, job performance. Assessing competencies at various points in time, establishing the presence and level or absence of specific competencies may occur in a number of ways. This study presents a methodology for efficiently implementing and managing competency assessment.

"Behavioral attributes" represent those aspects of personality that promote success in task execution. "Skills," on the other hand, refer to more operational, trade-like expertise that temper practical or technical knowledge with experience to establish a likelihood of satisfactory performance with regards to an assigned task. "Knowledge" most often refers to the accumulated academic experience that adds depth and the substance of historical insight to an expanding range of inputs, each contributing to an overall expertise directed toward a given task or outcome.

---

3 https://www.etymonline.com/word/compete?ref=etymonline_cross reference

Why, you may ask, do we require such a complicated explanation? Would it not be possible simply to consider skill as the predominant indicator and present a simpler indicator of competency? Unfortunately, the proposed paradigm requires a level of detail, a level of clarity for each element that enables a specific characteristic to present on its own merit, which, when joined with other characteristics, defines and determines the desired sub-competency or competency. This outcome does not allow for a simplistic approach to such a complicated challenge. In this case, skill and competency are complementary but not synonymous.

A skill is task-based, usually acquired through execution repeatedly and satisfactorily over time. A skill may be classified as "hard," such as stitching shoes or forging armor, or "soft," such as the ability to market goods, and promote and secure the sale of shoes or armor. Each and both skill sets have tremendous value. Not surprisingly, the sum of these skills collectively represents a significant portion of an individual's value—their competency.

At this point, we might agree that "competency" represents the capacity and willingness of the competent person to introduce a skill to their mix of talents with consistent effect. The optimum result integrates an amalgam of an individual's best attributes in the form of soft and hard skills into the mix of capability directed toward an intended outcome.

Consider for example, a waiter serving coffee to a customer in a café. The waiter repeatedly interacts with customers utilizing his soft skills by presenting a welcoming attitude and performing at a high level of customer service. The ready acceptance by the customer enables the waiter to introduce the hard skills necessary for a complete and most satisfactory experience—the order, preparation, and presentation of the coffee . . . simple but effective.

The customer pleased with the interaction will most likely return again, perhaps even the next day and thereafter. This in turn will motivate café management to highlight or reinforce the behavior and expand it to the entire café staff. The action of reinforcement extends the behavior beyond this single event and creates a defined pattern of behavior, a standard practice desired of the entire café staff, intended to produce a similar outcome in every instance. Sharing this behavior among waiters expands the competency of each and collectively creates a competitive advantage for the café and improves the potential for a more profitable business for the owner. You will recognize the concept, perhaps in your own inventory of experiences, so it certainly is not new. In fact, several pioneers have already investigated the potential for introducing competency-based thinking into our daily lives.

COMPETENCY BASIS AS RECENTLY APPLIED TO LANGUAGE PROFICIENCY STANDARDS

The process of defining a standard tool to measure competency began in the 1960s under the auspices of the European

Cultural Convention, wherein member States of the Council of Europe proposed to assure that all motivated citizens have the opportunity to learn additional languages beyond their native first language.

Across four decades, the process evolved into the CEFR—Common European Framework of Reference for Languages. In November 2001, the European Union Council recommended using the CEFR to set up systems of validation of language ability. The six reference levels are becoming widely accepted as the European standard for both grading an individual's language proficiency and for extending the standard beyond the EU.

Within the framework, there are three main features that collectively result in a determination of competency. The first, Mastery, enables the demonstration of skill and content knowledge sufficient to certify a candidate as competent. Throughout the process, progress is paced to the individual needs, optimizing the learning style of the individual. Lastly, support is customized in order to produce a progressive and challenging environment capitalizing upon the individual optimum time frame.

Additionally, studies have introduced a competency grid for each language containing its structure and origin in order to further improve the outcome. Consider the French (continental) language. The source of European French, a mixture of *langue d'oeil* and *langue doc* before the French Revolution, evolved differently in many parts of the world and requires subtle attention to the spoken tongue. Each dialect is spoken with subtle differences in vocabulary, pronunciation, and written language. Manifesting a competency in each language requires a command of both aspects. For example, the dialect of French spoken in Quebec, Canada (Quebecois) is an amalgam of differences in spoken language, intonation, and residual 18th century vocabulary. Similar differences are apparent in the language culture of New Orleans (cajun, a corruption of "Acadien"). Additional subtleties of language exist in Belgian French as well. Specific competency assessment must measure each aspect in order to properly certify or recommend suitable talent for a specific challenge. In other words, specific competency is required for the proper delivery of language training, depending upon the venue of delivery and intent of the student.

As a more specific example, consider the case of the number eighty-four (84) in French. In France, the term is described as *quatre-vingt-quatre*, or "four times twenty [and] four." In Belgium or Canada, however, it is recognized and pronounced as "eighty-four." These differences must be recognized, acknowledged, and integrated into the assessment of competency in order to properly reflect local language subtlety. This is a critical requirement of a common framework.

The CEFR strives to establish a basis for delivering and measuring a process of mastering an unknown language by classifying the vehicle of competence under review such as: "Understanding," "Speaking," or "Writing," further classifying these into components or sub-competencies such as "Listening and Reading," "Spoken Interaction and Presenting," and "Writing"; using specific descriptors for each competence or sub-competence. These descriptors were introduced without specific reference to any individual language in order to improve applicability across a broad spectrum of languages and promote a more universal solution.

As defined, the descriptors are intended to reflect the depth and extent of progress achieved toward mastery of each competency. They are further classified into three levels:

1. "Basic User"
2. "Independent User"
3. "Proficient User"

Additional common reference levels are introduced to further facilitate recognition of language confidence measured on a six-level scale, including: A1, A2, B1, B2, C1, C2), referred to by CEFR as the Common Reference level. Here, the intent is to promote a transparent, coherent, and comprehensive basis for the sharing of language education:

1. syllabi,
2. curriculum guidelines,
3. design of teaching and learning materials, and
4. further assessing foreign-language proficiency

This methodology represents significant progress toward the establishment of a common approach to determining language competency.

In the CEFRL process, language competency process is divided into:

- Result Areas = Understanding, Speaking, Writing
  - Competencies = Listening, Reading, Spoken Interaction, Spoken Production, Writing
    - Sub-Competencies = Basic user, Independent user, Proficient user
    - Spoken language = Range, Accuracy, Fluency, Interaction, Coherence
      - Building blocks = A1, A2, B1, B2, C1, C2 (the proficiency levels)

The systematic breakdown into building blocks enables a narrowly focused, concrete, targeted-learning, and assessment goal-oriented process as the following model shows:

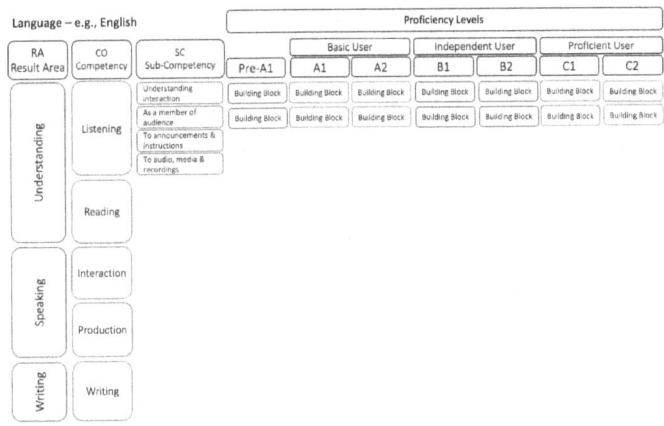

FIGURE 1: Competency Model Common European Framework of Reference (CEFR)

COMPETENCY-BASED ASSESSMENT IN EDUCATION

Also, in the 1960s, on the other side of the Atlantic, experimentation into competency-based education was evolving out of the behavioral-objectives movement proposing that "the norms and direction of education should come from the consumer aggregate, from society." Since then educational organizations around the world have contributed to the development of Competency-Based education.

In its current form, it represents an "approach that allows students to advance based upon their ability to demonstrate mastery of a skill and a willingness to improve competency at their own pace regardless of the environment. This self-directed methodology has proven somewhat effective in responding to the countless variants found in various learning abilities and have led to more effective and efficient learner outcomes.[4,5]

Consistent with most new processes, some criticism to Competency-Based Education has been raised, complaining that competency-oriented education fails to focus on personal development but targets mainly functional and task-oriented development. More research is required—beyond the scope of this article—to respond to this point. However, in short, this form of education has demonstrated an outcome that produces better employees but remains inconclusive regarding the development of the individual. More work needs to be done, consistent with any new process with great potential.

Unfortunately, a continuing focus on job description-based talent fulfillment may actually mask the potential value of this program. Selection of associates according to their suitability for a specific task set consistent with current practice may enable an enterprise to fulfill the most basic minimum requirements of the moment but lose visibility into a much more important or expansive talent resource of potentially greater value in short-, medium- and long term.

An innovative approach to a resolution of this problem was begun in 2011 in the Netherlands, whereby a profession-oriented qualification structure was introduced. The

---

[4] https://www.gettingsmart.com/2017/12/competency-based-education-definitions-and-difference-makers/
[5] https://aurora-institute.org/

exercise did cause some confusion as the exercise reoriented the exercise from competence-oriented qualification to profession-oriented qualification. A key presupposition was superimposed over the exercise . . . that individual competency optimization already exists in markets and that talent-level standards by profession are a current reality. It is an unfortunate reality that either and both are not currently reflected in today's world. But that does not lessen the need to effect appropriate change.

US education proponents continue to pursue a path toward Competency-Based Education, and it has been suggested that, throughout the process, students gain flexibility to progress at their most suitable rate, allowing them to demonstrate mastery of academic content according to individual need for time, place, or pace of learning.

Competency-based strategies provide flexibility in the way that credit can be earned or awarded and provide students with personalized learning opportunities. Vehicles for learning and establishing competencies include online and blended-learning processes, dual enrollment and advanced credit courses in high schools, project-based and community-based learning, and life credit for experience, to name only a few.

This type of learning leads to better and more regular student engagement because the content is relevant to each student and tailored to their unique needs and talents. The result is generally better student outcomes, because the pace of learning is customized to each student. By enabling students to master skills at their own pace, competency-based learning systems help to save both time and money.[6]

ADAPTING COMPETENCY-BASED ASSESSMENT TO MARKET NEEDS

Although competency-based business-management practices have been in place for at least three decades, there is no uniform approach in their meaning, definition, integration, or structure in businesses or organizations. Several business and governmental organizations struggle to find "a" or, more precisely, "the" common ground on how to adopt competency-based employment.

Organizations define competencies independently of each other based solely on their own culture, industry relevance, and perception of the person who articulates the competencies. If then these ideas are tight to the industry and well-articulated, these ideas find adherence and conclude a new approach within the organization. For instance, leaders of a company with old-line manufacturing will more likely talk about very task-based—almost "scientific-management-based competencies." This one-sided view leads to an inaccurate and changeable translation and application of competency. A multitude of perceptions of

---

6 https://www.ed.gov/oii-news/competency-based-learning-or-personalized-learning

competency has led to today's ambiguity in the evaluation of organizational processes.

Some organizations believe in three types of competencies that are considered important for their employees. These three types are:

- Core competencies
- Functional competencies
- Cross-functional competencies

Other organizations believe in a different structure and describe competencies in generic terms, such as "things" that an individual must demonstrate in order to reveal effectiveness in a job, role, function, task, or duty. These "things" include job-related behavior (what a person says or does that results in good or poor performance), motivation (how a person feels about a job, organization, or geographic location), and technical knowledge/skills (what a person knows/demonstrates regarding facts, technologies, a profession, procedures, a job, an organization, etc.).

These organizations apply their approach to competencies through a study of tasks and roles that leads to a conclusion that competency is the sum of:

- Abilities
- Attitudes

- Education (applied)
- Languages (use)
- Experience (applied)
- Skills (learned) categorized as behavioral, functional, technical, operational

Labor process analysis is replete with competency grids measuring function, position, or domain and further reported by subclassifications deemed important to the organization. Indeed, *that which is measured is addressed.* However, it is more suitable that the elements measured justify the cost and result in an outcome of great value to the organization. Measuring twice and cutting once is a mantra of good carpentry. In organizations, the exercise of measurement should result in the best possible and timely information in support of objectives.

Systems have been created to help organizations frame their own staff and allow targeted performance reviews and professional training. Several learning-and-development business leaders have voiced concerns regarding the ineffectiveness of their learning-acquisition and -assessment methods. The purpose, timing, and very content have been perceived as inconsistent and not particularly effective.

The process of selecting and developing an enterprise's talent is in need of upskilling. The current methodology leads generally to misalignment with the overall corporate objectives, and these have become supported by archaic and ineffective performance measurements. Competencies, motivation, and objectives must be aligned in order to assure business growth and competitive advantage, regardless of industry or market.

Organizations focused on fulfilling the limits of job-description hiring stand supported by standard periodic performance reviews that measure achievement of fixed objectives tied to the job description. In many organizations, these reviews occur at the end of the third month of a new hire and annually for staff employees.

Better than *no* review, this practice provides some insight into the acceptability of the job as defined in the hiring job description. The delimiting factor becomes apparent once the employee evidences a capability that transcends the limits of the job description. If allowed to pursue a broader agenda, an employee often brings additional competencies to the enterprise, thus expanding the contribution in ways not measurable by current standards at the point of hire.

The key lies in identifying the under- or non-recognized competencies as the initial evaluation of the potential new hire. This challenge is compounded by a lack of training or experience in identifying these diverse talents. The process of optimizing talent is further complicated by a general lack of experience in suggesting or directing the motivated employee toward challenges that, though they may extend beyond the job-description brevet, would further motivate the talented employee and add significant value to the enterprise in both the short and longer term. Lastly, the reviewer is faced with a clash of conscience, weighing his mandated objectives and a loyalty to assist the employee to develop.

Research provided by Stanford University and Gallup analytics suggest that performance reviews have become outdated for the pace of today's markets and have become less appropriate for evaluating and guiding employees in their own and the best interest of the enterprise[7].

APPLYING A COMPETENCY-BASED METHOD TO BUSINESS/ ORGANIZATIONAL MANAGEMENT

A competency-based approach in education has already yielded valuable insight into its value with regard to child education, particularly in the area of language-skill development. Might we consider the adoption of similar techniques in non-educational organizations? With the growing body of knowledge surrounding the value of this new area of development, should we not conclude that there is a need to extend investigation and implementation into the business process?

Should the next step taken be to introduce a series of common definitions enabling all interested parties

---

[7] https://www.gallup.com/workplace/249332/harm-good-truth-performance-reviews.aspx

to evaluate and operate on common ground, thus facilitating a faster growth curve both in process acceptance and business results? The work has already begun, as previously noted in the discussion of the CEFR in the European Union.

Might we capitalize upon the tremendous effort already expended in order to adapt a business-focused solution through which to introduce a competency-based solution?

Many of the steps in that direction have already been introduced in the business process. An executive leader and change agent will already recognize the myriad of paths already implemented but in a disparate manner. Business-process management identified desirable steps to effect an optimum solution, driven by scientific methodology. Various other approaches have touched upon the use of emotional quotient in order to identify the best customer-management processes and methodologies to create competitive advantage.

All added somewhat to the improvement of outcome for the enterprise but depended upon the level and extent of interest promoted by the enterprise. Results were enjoyed according to the level of interest. And the improvement remained only so long as the change agent retained his direct interest in driving the process.

Introducing competency-based business process integrates itself into the corporate DNA and becomes organic to the enterprise and continuous, without the need for specific direction or even guidance.

To realize this success, an initial review of business processes is in order. Business-process mapping assures efficient operations driven by the best range of activities, streamlined, cohesive, and effective, with the outcome providing the most value from the enterprise factors available. A particularly beneficial starting point for such investigation is the Order-to-Cash Cycle, defined by the domain bounded from point-of-order to cash conversion of the invoice. The value to the enterprise is most obvious and provides a solid return on investment . . . a good place to begin.

Variously referred to as the Order to Cash Cycle, the Invoice to Cash Cycle, etc., the processes support maximum profitable selling and customer-portfolio development. A more granular review of the processes identifies the historical business functions of: Order Management, Credit and Invoice Collection Management, Distribution (Order Pick, Pack, and Ship), Customer Invoicing, Accounts Receivable, Cash Application, Account Reconciliations, Reporting, Measurement, and Data Management. Each is classified individually as a Result Area.

These Result Areas, generally already in place in most organizations in one form or another, provide a basis to measure current efficiency and comparative results of the change in performance.

Applying a process similar to the CEFRL, these major Result Areas (competencies, if you will) are further dissected into their operational components (sub-competencies) to include technical, functional, operational, and behavioral dimensions.

Assessing process proficiency (individual) or efficiency (process), the outcome is classified as: Limited Proficiency, Developing Proficiency, Proficient, or Highly Proficient, providing for a systematic methodology for improving the outcome. It is a process that has seen success in its CEFRL form and can be adapted to business processes, as, for instance, for the Order to Cash Cycle, the O2C:

The elements of the O2C include:

- Result Areas = Order Management, Credit Management, Order Fulfillment, Shipping, etc.
  - Competencies = Customer Creation, Credit Risk Management, Order Entry, Cash Posting, etc.
    - Sub-Competencies = Functional, Technical, Operational, Behavioral
      - Building blocks = Proficiency levels (Limited, Developing, Proficient, High)

The standardization of competencies and required definitions as developed and applied to each Result Area enables the program to overcome normal project inertia and accelerate outcomes. Simultaneously advancing both human and process resources will yield faster results in a lower-risk, controlled environment. Designed to progress according to the business condition and employee motivation, the competency-based approach introduces its value-add in an opportune and noninvasive way.

This system promotes organization competitive advantage through:

1. Releasing individual competency constraints of current systems
2. Fostering individual development with flexibility
3. Providing organizations with current inventory of competencies (recognized and utilized, under- or non-utilized and available)
4. Enabling a strategic view of capacity and organizational needs
5. Measuring achievement at required operating levels
6. Identifying capacity gaps according to organizational needs (current and projected)
7. Identifying training and support needs to fulfill enterprise destiny
8. Aligning the corporate culture with its business strategy

Following the same pattern as the CEFRL process, once a common ground is established and process definitions agreed upon, the detailed "building blocks" may be finalized and stored as the ultimate creation of one single **library of building blocks** per business process accessible by *everyone*—a library as a database where all granular building blocks are tagged with name and barcode per business process.

The execution of these steps will enable an enterprise to systematically review processes, coordination of processes, and human resources to assure alignment and optimized outcome.

Once certified complete, both should enable a more fluent and informative business operation and assure competitive advantage for the enterprise. A related benefit results from the marginalizing of common areas of business conflict, such as gender, age, religion, etc.

Besides benefiting the business world, this model allows vocational and educational institutions to tap into this broad library of granular building blocks and use it effectively in their training and educational programs. Therefore, the question: "Are business leaders ready to agree on one, single common ground of competency-based business management and allow alignment with vocational/educational training?"

Encouraged by the rising GIG economy, many enterprises are adding shorter-term resources in order to meet certain demands. The same competency-based process will enable a much more productive solution in both areas: permanent and loyal associates of the enterprise as well as the GIG solution providers. In the end, it optimizes value in a more cost-effective manner.

Chapter 11

THE HISTORICAL PATTERN THAT LED TO THE CURRENT DILEMMA

During the course of explanation, the reader is reminded that a common vocabulary has been the enabler of productive business around the world. Definitions for terms such as business, employee, job, position, title, position description, hierarchical structure, organigram, competence, and proficiency levels, amongst others, have all served to ease the challenge of understanding those aspects of business that enable productive and profitable growth across markets. These same benefits created an organizational responsibility to set a strategy that, when properly executed, resulted in goal achievement . . . and success. In some ways, this archaic model persists in rudimentary form in the suggested paradigm . . . but with some major enhancements.

There are many extant examples that suggest types of challenges and case analyses that describe a strategy resulting in success. These include: the pharmacist's experiment that became Coca Cola, the supply chain dynamics of

Amazon, Google, and Adidas, the branding success such as Kellogg's Cornflakes, to name only a few.

All these companies introduced key innovations beginning with a single innovative idea as a one-(wo)man-show and rose to their current status as major multinationals employing thousands of people and providing income and health for a great number of families around the world. Key questions of importance include:

- How have resource needs been secured in the past?
- Have the volume and increasing speed of economic growth forced a reliance upon the status quo in HRC management?
- Despite obvious cost pressure across time, have entities merely relied upon rebalanced Income Statements to resolve fiscal outcome, without addressing core issues?
- Do these attitudes and solutions remain, and does this model suggest a viable alternative?

EVOLVING THE BUSINESS

Let us begin with a question: "What does the term 'Business' truly mean?" The definition found in common dictionaries derives from the Old English "bisignis," meaning "anxiety." The word "business" has a long history in Germanic languages, with the earliest words having meanings along the lines of "worry," "apprehension," or "concern" and the activity to avoid it. This left the old English to develop the concept into "bisignis" or later "busy-ness," meaning the condition of being busy (thus avoiding the devil's use of idle hands). This has allowed us to call a business a "concern" in many contexts, particularly legal ones, without thinking about the exact connection to the word "business." Western Bankruptcy law discusses a viable business as a "going concern" in precisely this context. The Germanic tribes, who remained on the continent after the Anglo-Saxons left, evolved the same root words into the modern German "Besorgnis" (concern or worry), with the similarity clear.

It further evolved through the 18th century to include the concept of busy-ness, the condition of being busy, expanding its meaning to represent tasks regularly executed with a common objective, now referred to as the "Job." The concept of a "job" was introduced around 1650 by Samuel Johnson in his dictionary and defined as "a low, mean, lucrative busy affair" and "Petty, piddling work."[8]

"Work" and "labor" are closely related words across all the various European languages. The Romans were the leading power and, in Latin, *laborare* means "great effort in service of a greater meaning." In most romance languages (all apart from Italian), the original meaning is a much darker one. It is pretty obvious who the designers and managers for the building of the aqueducts were and

---

8 https://www.etymonline.com/word/job

who the workers were. In French, for instance, the word for work is *travailler*, which has its origins in a device used to constrain (and torture/punish) slaves. This gave the original meaning of "work" in those languages a much darker meaning, more akin to "torture," "punishment," or "brutish effort." The workers clearly took a darker view of work than the leaders. It certainly has an impact upon how people regard work today when it recalls images of punishment.

For Germanic peoples, "work" meant something very difficult and wearying, more akin to "labor," indicating greater exertion in performance. The similar concepts of forced or brutish labor in Slavic tie to the modern German word for work, *arbeiten*, but arrive in English via the same source as "robot." This was coined in the 1920s from the Czech word *robota*, which was originally the forced work owed by a serf to the lord every year. Given its inheritance from Germanic, Latin, and Romance languages, modern English contains all of these many nuances to those words. A "job" was initially defined in English in Samuel Johnson's dictionary in 1755 as a "low" or vulgar word for similar brutish effort. What began as slang has morphed into wider use in the modern world. Across time, in constant use, the term has come, in the 21st century, to encompass a broader meaning to include "the principal activity in one's life executed in order to earn money," a source of personal and familial sustainment.

A "job" is for the present. A "career" is a sequence of jobs trending in one or more definable directions. We will discuss all this in more detail in a moment.

Take, for example, the cordwainer or shoemaker of the Middle Ages. Adequately performing his trade, he might individually be able to produce a single pair of shoes over the course of 16-hour workdays in a week or two, depending upon the style. However, should this tradesman desire to increase his revenue and stock, he was required to supplement his effort with that of an apprentice, often a family member.

Further growth often resulted in specialization of talent to introduce a higher level of expertise, which enabled the shop to attract a more-desirable clientele. Apprentices were delegated lower-level tasks until their demonstrated skill warranted greater responsibility. Ordinarily that commitment represented a five-year learning and production experience.

Journeyman tasks often included cutting leather to fit the customer size, producing sole, sewing, gluing, and nailing the shoe, inserting the straps or laces, with the employee presenting the final product to the employer for acceptance and final sale to the customer.

In this way, the employer was able to assess not only the quality of the end product but the overall proficiency of the employee or apprentice. Future tasks were assigned to each assistant based upon their demonstrated productivity or value to the employer, resulting in the recognition of specialization as a distinct value to the business. The division of labor was born.

In later days, such divisions of labor became contractually formalized as employers expected and compensated employees for the execution of specific tasks at particular levels of outcome. The description of those features became memorialized to assure common understanding of mutual expectations in task and objective performance. In that way, the "job description" was born. The degree of importance and value that the job held in the eyes of the employer was reflected in the title, responsibility, and salary offered to an acceptable candidate. The modern job description was born.

In the shoemaker's shop of the earlier age, the job description was simple and more obvious, often presented in the form of a discussion with a potential employee of the tasks to be accomplished, which might have included pattern transfer, sole shaping, cutting, or sewing—all tasks that should be accomplished in order to warrant a daily or weekly wage.

The more effective the shoemaker's team, the more goods were produced, with additional sales booked. As production expanded, employees were added, and the increased workload was distributed among employees. Growth required a more effective onboarding process and better coordination of the workforce to assure basic skill and process satisfaction, and to evaluate productivity and results in order to distribute tasks appropriately, in the interest of maximizing the value of all factors of production and trade. The process was largely unchanged as time evolved.

HOW HAVE RESOURCE NEEDS BEEN SECURED IN THE PAST?

Since the dawn of time, we have sought to give meaning to our lives. After the search for spiritual answers, we tend to look to work for meaning. Given it consumes most of our time and is the source of our most basic security, work has a central place in our sense of ourselves, our societies, and how we choose to grow and evolve.

The history of our work life, and our view of it, may be traced in rather amazing detail with the etymological shifts of the very words with which we seek to describe the business environment. Words like "work," "labor," "job," "hire," and "business" have a long linguistic history dating back well before the Anglo-Saxons to early Germanic and early Italic. A journey through the etymology shows a bit of the history as well as some of the cultural biases of former times—biases we carry with us into the present without realizing it.

The word "career" is derived in Latin from a type of chariot and arrived at its more modern meaning during the days of Napoleon. It has been since the "flow" of one's work life or maybe a collection of jobs in a particular direction.

Today, one sees a *job* as more task based and less long term than a *career*, and sometimes distinctions are drawn.

Another very commonly used business word is the word "Hire," in old English written "Hyr," and in old German was *Hüren*, with the meaning of "contracting for services." The meaning was entirely short term in concept and transactional in nature. The modern Dutch word *huren*, from the same root, has the precise meaning of "to rent." When the English say "hire car" today, it carries precisely its original meaning. This older meaning has not fully left us and still is part of our modern thinking. The original concept of "hire" was much closer to the modern slang "GIG," while businesspeople have argued for decades about the common perception that we fail to "hire" for the long term. Our modern difficulties are certainly reflected in how we misuse this word. One must wonder if our confusion does not unduly impact what a CEO mght describe as a major worry: the ability to obtain and retain talent to fuel their growth strategies.

Our modern language is rich in its ability to describe nuance and detail in business. But we are also more than a bit trapped by meanings and history in our words. This history is not fully apparent, but it is still present and leaves us with a range of nuance to the most basic vocabulary that we use to describe the environment which consumes roughly half of our waking lives. We build on threads of words and scraps of history to weave a work life that hasn't led us where we wish to go. We have built barriers between our work and home lives, and craft still other pieces to bridge the gap—like stopping at the pub on the way home. Is it not time to rethink things?

The systems with which we currently lead and manage employees and candidates also has a long historical tail. It has its origins in the Middle Ages with its craft guilds and, in the intervening years and centuries, has evolved as the various forces have made change upon it. As with all things in human history, change has come in fits and starts, driven by technological shifts, societal changes, and leaps in information which made the old process increasingly less useful, until change had to occur.

During the course of the 14th century, the feudal system began to break down, driven by the cataclysmic changes brought on by the Black Death. Workers left their jobs in manors to remove to larger towns and cities in order to obtain better paying work, away from the control experienced in manor life. In order for the cities to accommodate the growing volume of these new workers, a system was needed to prepare them with training, manage them, and assure a basic level of competency for tradesmen aspiring to set up shop and vend goods.

The trade guilds, in place since the 12th century, were the structure developed to provide this new order. They created a system to structure and manage trade process, manage workflow, assure compliance with its regulations, and promote conformity to assure the successful conclusion of the hire or trade event. Guilds maintained a consistent and dependable high quality, market-regulated pricing, and a forum for dispute resolution such that it created a high barrier to competition and the best trading solution for merchants.

As a consequence, workers were directed, trained, and developed within a narrow process band within which they were trained and developed to demonstrate productivity and capability consistent with three stages: apprentice, journeyman, and, ultimately, the highest expertise, as master. Each stage of development required several years of demonstrated performance, after which the guild trainee was deemed experienced sufficiently to follow his own path as a guild member.

Consistent with the times, few training elements were written down to be studied unless created by the master for his apprentices and journeymen. It was impractical due to the cost of books and low literacy of the students. It remained for the master to determine how many years an apprentice must train in order to achieve an acceptable level of competence before entering journeymanship. A similar variable time in grade was assessed by the master until the journeyman was deemed capable of carrying out the full complement of trade requirements and could move forward on his own. Quality was controlled, output regulated, and training was accomplished—one on one.

The hiring system, such as it was, operated from the bottom up, with openings at the bottom of the organization, followed by a progression from laborer apprentice, craftsman, journeyman, and finally master.

GROWTH AND INCREASING SPEED OF ECONOMIES

The impact of growth and increasing speed of economies on the status quo of Human Resource Capital HRC [talent] management

This process functioned virtually unimpaired until the arrival of the printing press in the middle of the 15th century. In a few short decades, the price of books dropped drastically, Knowledge was expanded exponentially, and literacy grew rapidly. With the volume of available titles exploding and a new opportunity to acquire books in native languages versus Latin, literacy kept pace accordingly. Training and development stayed in guilds but was now enhanced by written works as well as formal written documentation of positions and titles. In the shoemaker's shop of the earlier age, the written documentation was simple and more obvious, often presented in the form of a discussion with a potential employee of the tasks to be accomplished.

The next quantum leap occurred at the onset of the Industrial Age, which began around 1775 and rapidly spread across the western world until, by the end of the 19th century, it had influenced work and trade in most western countries. Consider, for instance, New York City, whose population rapidly expanded from a population of 60,000 in 1800 to 3,425,000 in 1900, as a result of the massive industrial output growth built upon labor.

Into this massive economic disruption came Frederick Taylor, father of the scientific method and one of the very first management consultants. His theory of "Scientific Management," as it was later labeled, fit with the growing respect for science and engineering. For workers, the science focus had the effect of turning "craft"-based jobs into a sequence of repetitive and mundane task-based ones.

This represented a significant departure from previous guild training and workplace evaluation processes. In its place were a series of well-defined, rote, and sterile job descriptions with performance assessment directed to the task level. Training was largely accomplished on the job, with little formal process but a focus on consistent and accurate repetition of the task. After all, the purpose of the method was to take out variability and improve standardization in order to improve apparent efficiency. This method was very successful, with rapid efficiency improvements at the expense of worker morale.

Building upon the concept, Henry Ford was able to drive significant efficiency improvements using his assembly line. From 1910 to 1925, the cost of a Model T in current currency dropped from ~$24,000 to ~$4,000. In the 21st century, we might experience these type of price changes for new products but, at the time, it was innovative and truly unprecedented.

Scientific Management thinking carried through the world war years. The significant disruptions to society and to people's experiences during the war years drove a shift from scientific management toward a more documented, organized, and defined structure. By the early 1960s, scientific management began to be abandoned in favor of more worker engagement.

ENTITIES RELIED UPON REBALANCED INCOME

The hiring and training processes largely developed linearly under little pressure to change. Labor was plentiful, management had the upper hand, and dictates of the business took precedence over the needs of the individual. The "employment problem" was recognized only as the world began to recover from the war in the 1970s and globalization pressure increasingly stressed trade. Despite obvious cost pressure across time, entities have merely relied upon rebalanced Income Statements to resolve fiscal outcome without addressing core issues.

We need a long-term and global perspective to fully grasp our current employment environment. As with all the other areas of business life, large changes are afoot. Over the past four decades, the world economy has generated more than two billion jobs, more than were created during the previous four centuries. If this continues, it will create another 2.3 billion jobs during the next four decades.

The current anxiety in the West is similar to the United States as it passed through agricultural mechanization in the late 1800s. More than 4.4 million farm workers were displaced, generating double-digit unemployment and visions of a dismal future. These economic transitions had real-world costs, as lives were disrupted and visions for the future were changed. This was the start of the manufacturing explosion of the 20th century. The confluence of rising available labor displaced by the farms, rapidly expanding manufacturing productivity, and new product innovation produced a rapid pace of change.

Over the last 100 years, employment in the United States grew by almost 100 million jobs, or 400 percent. Between 1990 and 2005, it increased yet again by 23 million. During the last 15 years, total employment in the EU-15 rose by 26.6 million or 19 percent. The same pattern of structural transition and growth is repeating itself today and raising similar anxieties. Contrary to common wisdom, the total rate of US employment, the percentage of total US population with paying jobs, rose steadily throughout the 20th century from 38 percent to 46 percent and reached 48 percent by 2005.

It was impacted by the financial crash but recovered and, surely, has been impacted by the current coronavirus pandemic, but it will likely resume historic trends. We can expect that jobs will continue to grow at a rate higher than the population growth.

This suggests that the supply of skilled people will always be less than the demand. Processes such as "talent management" will have continued demand. The processes that we have adopted more recently—and their faults and errors—point the way to the needs of the future.

Developing countries have seen a slightly different path. Job growth has been quite rapid in the developing countries over the last forty years, more than doubling total employment. The single most important factor behind rising numbers of unemployed persons and increasing absolute numbers of families below the poverty line in developing countries has been the threefold expansion of population in the Third World. It has more than doubled over the general population since 1950, and resulted in a 4 percent decline in the overall employment rate. Population growth rates continue to fall steadily in most countries, providing an opportunity for economic growth and job growth to catch up with the population explosion of recent decades.

For instance, from 1950 to 2006, global population increased from 2.5 billion to 6.6 billion, a growth of 164 percent. During the same period, total global employment rose from 900 million to 2.9 billion, a growth of 222 percent. More recently, between 1996 and 2006, global population increased by 766 million or 13 percent, while total global employment grew by 400 million or 16 percent.

The unmistakable conclusion: a higher percentage of people are employed.

This background suggests a reason why we have arrived at this point in our economies. We tend to move the technological side of business faster and at the expense of the organizational side. The human and emotional foundation of our business world has not been designed by some "invisible hand," as Adam Smith suggested for another context. Rather, our methods of organizing have evolved from an intuitive response to the stresses that were placed on business over time. We typically place a patch on it and move on.

DO THESE ATTITUDES AND SOLUTIONS REMAIN, AND DOES THIS MODEL SUGGEST A VIABLE ALTERNATIVE?

Currently, everyone involved in the hiring, retaining, learning, and development process agrees, either explicitly or tacitly, that the process is completely broken. From the job seeker who hides flaws or gaps in his background to the employer who does not have a complete picture of what she truly needs, the process is at best a collection of partial solutions, Band Aids, and workarounds that has a very low success rate. In fact, if our air travel had a similar success rate as the hiring process, no one would fly.

The current process has huge costs for business as well as wasted effort from our educational institutions. In recent years, the top fifty talent-search firms alone booked revenue of $3 billion. Despite, and perhaps of a result of the current pandemic disruption, the trend will continue to extend. The demand for key competencies remains, and the selection process that identifies and most beneficially utilizes these talents will prevail in markets. To a significant degree, this industry can be seen as "waste" in our current system for hiring and retaining competent employees. Its size gives us a sense of the significant magnitude of the costs that might be avoided. The point is not to paint an entire industry in a negative light; the search industry performs a vital role in making business function as a competent resource pool to fill gaps in a business structure, and it will always exist. It is simply to show that we pay a significant cost for the broken system that we currently have.

This book will provide a fundamental rethink of the rationale that once supported current structures of organizations. By providing a common table of definitions and a basic framework for discussion, this new model will offer a methodology toward a new construct for even the most basic business processes.

Chapter III

CURRENT MODEL FOR SECURING HUMAN RESOURCES

The present methodology for populating a talent pool continues to be driven by the demand assessment of both entity and market. Regardless of whether the entity is a commercial enterprise, government institution, or other body, within markets, they determine their capacity to satisfy market and customer needs and respond by establishing process flows to meet these needs. Generally, these consist of specific functions executed in an appropriate fashion to achieve competitive outcomes, among which is an acceptable level of continuing growth. Reliance is placed upon both human and process capital resources to enable that achievement.

HOW THE CURRENT MODEL DIFFERS IN FORM FROM HISTORICAL METHODS

As markets and customer needs continue to change, leaders have been compelled to analyze organizational and functional structures in an attempt to satisfy demands.

While some enterprises thrive, many more suffer periodic shocks driven by mismatches between needs and need satisfiers. Often this is the result of a talent pool that is mismatched to the demands of the entity and the fact that many entities continue to grow their talent pool based upon an outdated framework.

Contrast current needs with the following case. Consider a shoemaker, a master tradesman with responsibility for the highest-quality competitively deliverable to customers. Market forces lead to diversification and specialization of tasks and the utilization of apprentices to enable a deconstruction and division of the work, to train talent, and enable apprentices to shoulder some of the tasks in the production process.

Since it was the sole responsibility of the owner/master tradesman to assure a high-quality work product, he was motivated to ensure that each of his apprentices possessed the critical competencies and was constantly on the alert for those unique individuals who demonstrated additional, desirable skills/competencies that might be introduced to improve the product and differentiate the shoemaker from his competitors. Success in the form of growth further necessitated the introduction of new and more effective methods to profitably expand business. At best, this model was hit-or-miss.

Today when an entity (company or institution) decides to expand its footprint or establish a new presence, it goes through a familiar cycle, identifying by functional area what additional resources, most notably, human resources, are required to execute successfully. The starting point is usually an assessment of the current organization, management, and functions, and a determination of additional need, driven by job descriptions, expected to offer the best chance of success. If current operational levels are satisfactory to meet the additional demands, and if objectives are being met, there is generally only a supplemental analysis done to determine what *additional* resources/skills are required.

This picture presents a skills pool that is neither flexible nor efficient. Decision-makers labor under a burden of inadequate information, misinformation, hidden value, and conjecture. All parties acknowledge that the process is imperfect but deemed immutable, and simply carry on. Businesses typically favor hiring, usually perceived as a lower expense, over accepting the burden of developing talent.

Clearly, this attitude discounts the value of exposure to corporate culture, associate and organizational collaboration, and experience of associates in the training, interaction, and task-execution process. Generally, this oversight is reflected by a suboptimum value chain . . . and bottom line.

JOB-DESCRIPTION BOUNDED, SPECIFIC-JOB ORIENTED, AND DELIMITING

Admittedly, this short-term focus represents a lesser immediate expense. However, it also represents much less value to the enterprise, on a continuous basis. The better price-performance solution considers value improvement across time and suggests that a better value introduces specific expertise as required, makes this expertise known and available across a broader platform of need, and maintains the expertise, further developed within the entity family of organizations.

Simply, talent vetted and hired, integrated into the entity knowledge pool, becomes a growing distributed resource, consistently improving, with a capacity to utilize the resource across a broader spectrum of need. Clearly the longer-term solution provides the better price-performance value. The optimal solution encourages an entity to secure outside talent where required or to refresh the knowledge pool on a schedule optimal for the entity, further developing much of the entity competence in-house. The inclusion of this process in entity strategic planning further promotes a broader utilization of potentially scarce resources, further contributing to the competitiveness of the entity. This is a value-over-value proposition and a price-performance driver as the entity competes in markets.

Most entities approach hiring, development, and retention as a secondary exercise, the decision having been made to introduce the associate into the pool of talent. Even in the best of markets, costs spiral as new hires are introduced and their actual and potential contributions suboptimized, in the process expending huge amounts of capital. Recruiting in the US tallied almost $152 billion in 2019[9] and was projected [pre-pandemic] to drop 20% in 2020. The sheer size of the market and reporting suggest that entities worry they don't have the capacity to handle immediate—and certainly not future—needs. We suggest an alternative inventory of talent is required.

The typical description of need for human resource is outlined in the job description. Entities formulate and circulate to appropriate leadership a draft job description indicating a combination of necessary hard and soft skills. The job-description content is an amalgam of legal requirements, ideal satisfiers, and observations made by some few managers involved and then set into an approved format by the Human Resources group of the entity. It is an internal document intended to clearly state the essential job requirements, job duties, job responsibilities, and skills required to perform a specific role.

It is often divided into sections with clearly marked labels. In most instances, the requirements are the opinions of those involved and represent their experiences, desires, and biases in written form. There is little thought given to the daily business processes to which the role responds or to the actual business process skills that the person hired must possess over an unclear timeline. In short, it is, at best, an incomplete picture and, at worst, highly off the mark.

---

9 https://www.statista.com/statistics/873648/us-staffing-industry-market-size/

Several organizations have specialized in providing standard formats and have built directories containing job-description examples covering all the most popular or common roles. The templates can easily and quickly be downloaded and modified to suit unique business requirements. Starting with a sample job description, everyone will be able to complete all key requirements for a role, and new hires will have a better understanding of what their role is. Within a seven-step process, everyone within a company can write a job description and have it checked by the hiring manager or Human Resources department. We have efficiently gotten to the wrong destination faster.

PERPETUATING THE POOL WITH A FALSE EXPECTATION AND CONFIDENCE

In most cases, the employers are partnering with a recruiting agency. The recruiter takes this information, analyzes it, and interviews the hiring manager and, in some instances, only the responsible Human Resources agent, in greater detail. This uncovers some gaps that are corrected by a limited amount of new information. It does formalize and structure the hiring process somewhat, but it comes at a significant cost for the enterprise as information is reworked and more people are involved. But, crucially, the process begins with an *inadequate starting point*. The process gives very little attention to the actual competencies required or desirable; it only defines the work processes within which the role will be working and opines that the new hire fit in with reference to the existing team. This perpetuates the pool with a false expectation and confidence, with the risk of securing suboptimum, permanent resources and populating the HRC pool accordingly.

Why such an inadequate starting point? Perhaps it is the partial responsibility of the source that creates the job description. Who within a company describes and authorizes the content of a job description? From what source does the authorized title proceed? Who establishes hard- and soft-skill requirements for the position? Is the position newly created or existing? Is it the result of a recent vacancy? When a critical position opens up, the responsible hiring manager will almost immediately want to know how this vacancy is going to affect the organization and how quickly and effectively he or the company can fill this position. Is the hiring manager or the HR employee familiar with the culture and core values of the company and capable of translating them into a job description? Does the present budget still accommodate the vacated position?

Unfortunately, in most cases, salaries do not correlate to the educational and professional requirements of the job description but, at best, correspond to that approved for the title under consideration. How often does the title of a position match the requirements of a job description? Because of this ambiguity, most job descriptions avoid indication of salary. Considering the current experience of educational inflation, entities are generally overstating the requirements of open positions in the hope of attracting more highly educated and presumably more qualified talent. Given these considerations, is it unreasonable to conclude that the existing process of creating, posting, and securing applicants through the job description is anything but flawed?

INTERNAL AND EXTERNAL SELECTION BASED UPON INCOMPLETE, FALSE, OR IMPROPERLY CLASSIFIED CONTENT

The job description is usually broadcast on the job market via job boards, social media, and so on, looking for candidates. This is called "Trolling for Talent" or a "Post and Coast Strategy," flooding the job boards in the hope that the aspiring entity will identify that perfect fit and secure top talent for their open positions. One wonders how many new hires bring personal resources fully adequate for the job description for which they are being hired but totally suboptimum for the potential challenges for which they are *currently* prepared. Nevertheless, this strategy creates a database of available candidates actively looking for a new, more satisfying opportunity and seeking that satisfaction across a broad spectrum of applications to the job postings.

While this process provides the entity with an illusion of progress, it often merely fills the applicant funnel with large numbers of apparently marginal candidates. To their credit, some job boards and social media have already developed a skill-mapping technique that matches applicant CV with the requirements of open job postings as described in job descriptions posted. For instance, LinkedIn provides a skill rating on a scale from 0 to 10, offering a preliminary suitability indicator, matching entity job description to applicant profile, created by the applicant within the LinkedIn platform. Additionally, the match is subject to issues of actual experience, honesty, and ethical beliefs of the data-entry source and does not guarantee a more efficient result for the entity placing the job description or hiring potential for the applicant.

In a global survey (2019), recruiters complained of challenges as they prepared to confront the Next-Gen workforce. The review expresses that "Recruiters are confident. Candidates are high quality. And, yet, around the world, recruiters are struggling to fill positions," according to Monster's 2019 State of the Recruiter survey. Further, the report bemoans that, despite their confidence and a deep talent pool, 71 percent of recruiters indicate they struggle to fill positions because of candidate skill gaps. More than 80 percent of all 1700 candidates interviewed by recruiters exaggerate skills and competencies on their resume. While these candidates appear competent on paper, recruiters find it necessary to adjust [lower] expectations of the intended level of skills to find "a" right fit. Does this message warn only of puffery by applicants in skill-set assertion or a mixed message indicating a mismatch between job description (perceived need) and verifiable applicant satisfiers supporting actual need?

SUBJECT TO CAREER DESCRIPTION BY CANDIDATE [INFINITE VARIABILITY WITHOUT CONSENSUS]

The applicant or jobseeker, on the other hand, pursuing a posting or scrutinizing a job description presents personal marketing documents such as CV, professional resume, recommendation or motivation letter, education, and experience to encourage hiring-entity interest and influence selection. The fact that almost no information is cross-checked creates an ethical and honesty challenge and introduces an inherent risk in this applicant presentation process. Though inherently risky, the process may result in a more intimate interview, one that achieves the objectives of both parties, the face-to-face interview.

It is only at this point that both parties may begin to establish basic suitability for the task intended by the entity and which meets the objectives of the applicant. Simply, sharing more detail directly with the hiring resources of the entity enables an applicant to translate experiences, degrees, or certifications into a recognizable position with the appropriate approved title and description targeted to a specific organization chart and salary point. Realistically, this inefficient process represents an acknowledgment that *the hiring process is broken.*

Given these inadequacies, why would either the entity or the applicant market an inaccurate or incomplete picture of either? In the case of an applicant, depending upon one's personal needs and desires, they would be delimiting their potential to the indicators required by a job description. The question arises regarding how the applicant was drawn to the opportunity. Was it the title or the set of requirements? Was it perhaps the entity brand or name?

Regardless of the trigger, the framework for response remains controlled by the process selected by each hiring entity. The applicant must comply with the process or risk no consideration. There is little chance of aligning mutual objectives and, accordingly, of identifying competencies that are of considerable short-, medium-, and even long-term value to hiring entities.

The current process prevents an applicant of deep and diverse talent from showcasing these opportunities to potential hiring entities. The exercise becomes one of securing a suboptimal, entry-level position in the hopes of leveraging it into an opportunity of real value . . . or perhaps gaining selective expertise and experience to transfer with greater gain to the next entity (perhaps a competitor entity).

THE QUESTION OF ETHICAL CONTENT AS PRESENTED

Was the applicant interest piqued by position title, authority, or responsibility? Once the decision was made to apply, did it require tailoring of the resume or CV to more closely match the job descriptors? Does the owned skill level and experience match the descriptors? For better or worse, the key questions relate to whether or not the application will secure the necessary interview in order to showcase actual areas of importance, say, of maturity. Further, are there relevant facts that impact the suitability of the applicant that are important to the applicant?

Consider, for example, the case of a single mother who has raised her child for thirteen years, relying upon temporary positions. She is now in a position to secure full-time employment consistent with her degree or qualifications. In the current market and measurement system, it is difficult to present her quality, including the successes, responsibilities, and challenges overcome during the course of the last decade.

In fact, she will have managed through educational, organizational, and financial challenges and excelled in her professional and personal life. What vehicle enables the showcasing of these important competencies and skills to appropriately value this applicant? The very fact that this question is posed represents yet another shortcoming of the present system for human resource classification and appreciation.

CURRENT LEVEL OF SATISFACTION GIVEN CURRENT STATE OF SECURING, RETAINING, AND DEVELOPING RESOURCES

Some progress has been made in understanding and efficiently identifying the vagaries of human resource valuation. The most recent exercise, driven by the quest for competitive advantage, cost advantage, and the strategic inside track, has been the introduction of the twin concepts of "Talent Management" and "Talent Acquisition." These have added additional focus to the conversation if not a substantial solution to the challenge.

These companies and recruiters act within constricted parameters such as title, position description, budget, industry, culture, values, etc. These are components of a methodology used to generalize a possible fit, to select candidates deemed unsuitable at the first instance, and reduce the population, requiring further research, time, and expense. Again, we are confronted with parts of a whole, considered piecemeal, in an attempt to secure the best possible talent to fulfill entity needs.

The process of title inflation is, by itself, a serious negative factor in the optimum selection of talent for a particular required outcome. Though the attempt is valiant, at what cost does it come, and at what level of impairment to productive outcome? Does this not present a system destined to fail and result in an ineffective method for optimizing an entity critical success factor and most precious asset—its human capital—in fact, *you*?

In many respects, the human resource pool represents in aggregate the most critical success factor (CSF) of an entity. The introduction and promotion of an efficient onboarding process is an equally important step in efficiency. Optimizing effective evaluation, selection, regulation, and development of an agile population of suitable resources is a vital component of entity success, regardless of industry, entity, or market. It will take on an even more vital responsibility in the wake of the current pandemic.

Currently undefined and consequently unrecognized, the skills and competency inventory introduced by newly hired or—more importantly—by existing employees, if effectively accessed, represent tremendous value-add to an entity. Efficiency and timeliness directed to areas that refine or further improve features will better serve the entity. From the first moment, as these new hires begin to acculturate to the new space, the opportunities to perceive, evaluate, and discuss observations combine and, in some cases, conspire to question the status quo and add further value to entity outcome. In the end, a successful hiring and development program secures growth and competitive advantage for the business.

Growth stimulates an internal need for organization structure to assure management control in pursuit of business objective, usually maximum profitable trade. Aligning business elements within the business requires designated authority and responsibility, and the measurement of same. In simpler times, perhaps with our shoemaker, it was the sole responsibility of the master tradesman to assure high-quality work product.

Growth, that passage of time and influence of markets, has necessitated the introduction of new and more effective methods to profitably expand business.

POSSIBLE OPTIMIZATION OF THE HRC?

Whether optimization is even possible, given the gaps in characterization of the HRC and as a consequence of the entire permanent resource pool

In this modern age, it is no longer acceptable or economically efficient to employ factors that do not perform up to the level of their potential. New equipment is introduced that is more efficient, requires less energy and maintenance, and produces output at multiples of predecessor machines.

Similarly, the human resources now represent opportunities to improve the actual economic value of each hire both initially and as they demonstrate a contribution to the growth of the business.

Creating an environment that selects talent, establishes previously untapped resources within the employee, and directs that value toward areas of specific importance to the business results in an accelerated organic and profitable growth. Further, it encourages loyalty by stimulating motivated employees to recognize and be recognized for the contribution.

The control or management requirements of growth benefit from a more stable, loyal, and accountable population of employees, managers, and leaders who, as a result of their improved [productive] longevity, can convey a more stable business more competitively across sometimes-volatile markets. Clearly, this represents a win-win condition.

Human resources are factors of service or production. In order to best benefit an entity, they require both a willingness to function within an environment that effectively utilizes talents both recognized and unrecognized to raise levels of satisfaction [desirably *delight*] in which they hold a relationship within the entity. Past experiences have demonstrated that merely conveying a sense of some level of previous capability and/or a willingness to take on the challenge as described in a particular job description is no longer sufficient to justify the hiring of a resource.

Compound this complex issue with an economy that not only prevents addition of permanent resources but eliminates the potential to retain certain key assets. Is it any wonder that turnover, both intended and unintended, rose so egregiously over the recent past, further complicating the challenge of entity growth or sustainment?

Challenged markets and production targets under stress have forced business to stretch the understanding of productivity to include a review of the human resource factor in order to introduce more and better utility and output from this value. *More with less* will remain a mantra for some years to come. We must rise to the challenge with a more efficient solution.

Extracting more value from a given resource, especially the complicated human resource, requires a look at production and satisfaction from both viewpoints: employer and employee. The entity requires a capability to execute tasks in order to produce an output in an acceptable time frame at an acceptable cost. This is all well and good in a static environment, where process is stable and there is little variable change. This is clearly not the case of trade, local or global.

Further, tasks have been relegated to silos described in fixed ways as enumerated in job descriptions, with acceptable behavior confined to achieving targets tied to narrow administrative objectives. I refer the reader to any job description for evidence. The rote execution of historical process often adequately serves the immediate needs of the hiring business segments, producing customer sales, expeditious billing, timely conversion of invoices to cash, etc. The aggregate of these fulfilled job descriptions constitutes the base of most human resource pools.

FROM WHENCE TALENT MANAGEMENT SYSTEM (TMS) AS CONCEPT?

As previously introduced, the concept now commonly known as "Talent Management" was first discussed in research done by McKinsey in the late 1990s and subsequently expanded over the next decade to include *War for Talent* (ISBN: 9781578514595). Discussion resulted in the expansion of the idea throughout the business community that human resources were a strategic value to the entity. As such, these assets required duty of care similar to other fiscal and physical assets of the entity.

Similarly, the organizational strategy, which all organizations possess, whether written or oral, demands the support of certain talent in certain quantities at certain venues in order to execute a common strategy and assure the success of the entity. This elevated the discussion of Human Resources from the back office to the Executive Offices.

Further introduction of the Talent Management concept gave rise to new descriptors such as "Talent Acquisition," "Talent Retention," and "Talent Development." All of these are pieces of the overall Talent Management System. As consideration of the concept expanded, these terms were introduced to ensure focus on the components of the program, perhaps more marketing than substance. But if they improved the potential for success, what harm is done?

Not unusually, it was among the largest entities, major corporations, that funding was approved to evaluate and fund the program. A large base of consulting companies rose to facilitate the project that integrated the concept through various software solutions with entity main operational control systems, initially mainly SAP and Oracle.

Proponents of the Talent Management approach argue:

- It pulls together formerly disparate components into a strategic whole
- It is a logical, cost-effective way to enhance workforce productivity
- It links directly to the overall strategy approved by the Board
- It is to what HR should aspire

Much has been accomplished over the last decade, with near-universal acceptance of the concept of Talent Management as well as the rationale supporting its strategic importance. Less acceptable is the comparatively high entry cost to the organization of the process and the integration cost of the various software. One commonly hears, "There must be a cheaper way" when discussing this with CEOs and Board Members. The comparative analysis and due diligence alone are a significant expense.

Prevailing arguments opposing implementation of the concept of Talent Management include:

- The process is focused on managing organizational star versus all human resources
- It is an 80/20 approach to people that mitigates the team objective

- Doesn't generally manage "Talent" but—at best—20% of available pool
- Ethical complications cloud the Talent Management message
- Produces bloated costs and buzzwords with poor results
- Merely an expensive "relabeling" of HR

Additional counterarguments include:

- Talent is not holistically identified, classified, assessed, and developed; this is inefficient
- Catastrophic change can happen without warning (e.g., Covid), and systems must be ready
- The TMS is inherently isolated from other areas of the business
- Potential, talent availability, and competence are neither synonymous nor mutually exclusive features

Talent Management has encouraged acceptance of the need to harness organizational skills, knowledge, and abilities to execute a successful organizational strategy. A key difficulty in its presentation evolves from the fact that it stems from a flawed premise. An objective of developing 20% of a workforce overlooks the fact that 80% of the competencies reside in that outlier population.

Fundamental to this 80/20 split of attention is the quiet conclusion that it is simply too costly for an organization to focus on everyone; as a matter of organizational sanity, some choices need to be made. This assumption has led the entire Talent Management process astray.

A consequence of the TMS is the Applicant Tracking System that represents a codified, automated, AI-enhanced tracking system for applicant's CV and analyzes and vets each in a structured and legally defensible manner. Since it has become a gatekeeper, there is now a cottage industry for writing and managing the CVs so that they fare well within the ATS. The candidates who are normally presented for review are only the ones whose CVs have successfully run the gauntlet and arrived at a reviewer's desk. On one hand, this is certainly more effective, but it interjects little to improve the overall efficiency of the human resource pool.

Now, enterprise economic challenges and the continuing quest for competitive advantage suggest the need for a new solution to optimize enterprise value and success. The truly successful enterprise will be the one that extracts the *full value of competencies* resident within, or to be selected by, the enterprise.

Organizations need to be ready to adjust on a moment's notice. It is no longer sufficient to be simply agile. Consider that two footballers possessing equal physical characteristics may show vastly differing abilities to intuitively adjust in real time to a play and execute a crucial score. The more capable is said to possess better "Twitch" muscles or response time at speed from the first step. We describe an organization with the same general differentiating characteristics as *twitch-agile*, or better prepared to spring forward and thus execute a better outcome.

Today's entity of acceptable agility will continue to compete but may be at a loss to prevail against competition for highest performance. The next stage of development requires a leap toward the *twitch-agile* level of performance, wherein all human capital resources are recognized and optimized, and deficiencies resolved in order to ensure maximum flexibility. Markets will require it, and stakeholders will demand it. They will be required to demonstrate the ability to rapidly reconfigure on the fly to combat new threats and to react to rapidly evolving change. This is true both in a macroscopic sense (reconfigure to external threats and opportunities) and also in a microscopic sense (reconfigure following a departure or accommodate short-term internal needs—GIGs).

A full accounting of organizational competence needs (as opposed to current or proposed strategy) requires treating the internal competence pool as an asset, with the respect and diligence any asset deserves. Potential new hires should be evaluated and assessed against those same needs.

It is clear that the near-term future world of work will be much more "GIG" focused. Internally, employees are rapidly deployed and redeployed to meet changing business needs. Externally, emerging various GIG-oriented resources will become available to supply a short-term, cost-effective, project-oriented solution free of part of the cost burden required of full-time headcount. This solution is expected to remain attractive as entities experience growth in overhead costs and as the model demonstrates growing economic efficiency.

Chapter IV

RETHINKING A PATTERN OF BEHAVIOR

INTRODUCTION OF A NEW COMPETENCY-BASED MODEL

Increasingly, the term "competency" has gained visibility in the current business vocabulary. Historically, it has described a condition wherein an individual has demonstrated an amalgam of knowledge, skill, and experience, the product of which represents a high-level command of the desired behavior. However, the *concept* of competency is often confused with the *elements that, in aggregate, result in the achievement* of a given competency. So how better might we understand competency? From what source is the term derived? Why does it now become important in the drive for competitive advantage in markets?

COMPETENCY AS IT APPLIES TO LANGUAGE PROFICIENCY

The original process, as previously mentioned, was created to standardize measurement and classification of language competency and introduced in 2001 as the Common

European Union Council Reference for Language [proficiency] or CEFR. The program has demonstrated its resilience, organic nature, and capacity to continuously adjust in order to maintain relevance and provide guidance in a fast-paced, high-demand world.

We have learned that the validation framework of CEFR offers a standard through which progression of competency develops through six reference levels from A1 to C2. Within the framework, there are three main features that collectively result in a determination of competency. First, Mastery provides visibility into skill and content knowledge at levels sufficient to certify a candidate as competent. Second, the process and progress are paced to optimize the learning style of the individual. Lastly, support is customized to produce a progressive and challenging environment enabling the best outcome within the optimum time frame appropriate for the individual.

CEFR bases determination of the level of mastery of a language by classifying Competency as: "Understanding," "Speaking," or "Writing" a language; further deconstructing these competencies into Sub-competencies such as Listening, Reading, Spoken language, Presenting and Writing. Each is measurable and represents the necessary enhancement to produce a higher level of competency leading to a full language competency. These descriptors were introduced without specific reference to any individual language in order to improve applicability across a broad spectrum of languages and promote a more universal solution.

Over time the model has adapted to different language contexts, adjusting to account for differences in learners and teachers/trainers, individual use, and cultural background. Further, the changes that the CEFR has seen lately move the CEFR process much more in line with the competency matrix suggested in this book. Consistent with the competency matrix, we would respectfully suggest adding a determinant for level of proficiency within each sub-competency as a means to measure and classify the actual level of expertise demonstrated by the person. This adjustment will contribute to an increase in the suitability of the competency designation.

The organic nature of the framework requires descriptors that continue to reflect the depth and extent of progress achieved toward mastery of each competency. In order to achieve that objective, an additional layer to the three levels of classification is also suggested.

To each level, additional granularity is suggested as follows: the first level, the "Basic User," it is recommended that additional levels be added. A1 and A2 would be further subclassified into A1.1 and A1.2 and A2.1 and A2.2, and so on as demonstrated in Figure 2 below.

The intent of the change is to expand the relevance of the framework into the academic community and enable recognition down to the smallest common denominator; our competency matrix suggests a slightly different approach, as shown below:

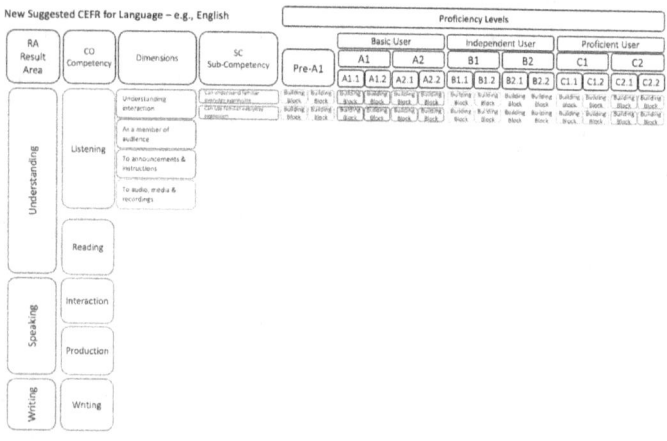

Figure 2: New Suggested CEFR for Language

The expanded features will promote a more transparent, coherent, and comprehensive basis for classifying and sharing the process of language education. The systematic nature of assessment of these component building blocks will enable more a narrowly focused, cocretely targeted learning and assessment, goal-oriented experience. The success of the current CEFR program attests to the significance of the process. The enhancement proposed by the rethinking proposed by the competency model in this book is intended to maintain research and dialogue going forward on this important topic of human capital development.

I. TOWARD A COMPETENCY-BASED APPLICATION FOR EDUCATION

Rethinking the Current Model

Particularly in light of the current global stress on education process, it behooves markets to pay particular attention to the methods and content introduced and conveyed to students in academic environments. Similar to other endeavors previously mentioned, beginning also in the 1960s on the Western side of the Atlantic, experimentation was begun into competency-based education. Taking a behavioral approach, it was suggested that "the norms and direction of education should take guidance from the client pool, the consumer aggregate, from society." Since then, educational institutions and organizations around the world have contributed to the body of knowledge required to develop competency-based education.

In the short term, the current method of education will continue to introduce improved graduates to markets, each of whom will have better comprehension and heightened ability to perform in their selected areas. Targeting objectives within markets as described by job banks and courted by Talent Management recruiters will continue to add some benefit to markets, even if that benefit is small and incremental to markets going forward. However, without a more innovative approach to the identification of competency and the fulfillment of need gaps in personal-talent inventories, this benefit to markets will remain suboptimal.

The paradigm focuses specifically on this shortfall and posits strong solutions.

The greatest benefit of a competency-based model requires a more innovative and comprehensive approach defining each relevant competency and further attaching key sub-competencies necessary to achieve performance at specified levels within specified dimensions.

Deficiency in designated areas as noted above will cause reversion to a series of developmental remedies to resolve missing content into the competency inventory of the individual. Similarly, this logic attaches to institutions and organizations, as each determines what expertise, knowledge, and performance standards they desire most, and following an assessment of their existing human resource pool, execute a strategy to introduce programs for resolving any deficiencies noted within the assessment time frame.

In current markets, little attention is paid to resident and desirable competencies in favor of job-description suitability. In this way, many possible options for optimizing existing talent are lost, and, worse, the potential forward-looking benefit of understanding these missing elements creates a continuing, suboptimal talent-utility mechanism.

The paradigm and supporting models introduced in this book focus specifically on shortfall resolution and posit a comprehensive solution to a continuing challenge, executing the best possible strategy with the best possible people in the manner most economically efficient.

In select US educational institutions, proponents experimented with aspects of competency-based education. It has been suggested that some improvement over the status quo is achieved through a self-paced learning process. This introduces additional flexibility in meeting academic requirements while engaging within time constraints more responsive to individual circumstances relative to time, place, capacity, and pace.

To better understand our premise, we offer the following:

Historically, students are presented with an assessment [report card] of their performance during the school term. The report summarizes their general success in subjects studied during the term usually by assigning a grade as an indicated level of success.

Typical subjects at lower grades include: mathematics, geography, history, and biology, etc., and success is assessed at the general topic level. The objective of the student is to acquire sufficient knowledge about the topic to pass a general exam on the subject. The content of each course, the curriculum at each level, and the exam core questions are introduced jointly by the state Ministry of Education and partly by the institution of learning.

Teachers introduce elements of their own style of teaching into the development of successful students and additionally rely upon recommendations and guidelines from the Ministry of Education and the respective school institute.

For example, referring now to the general subject of Mathematics, a student performance would be recorded according to their summary success on the subject. Students, parents, and teachers are conditioned to understand the system of A, B, C, D and the relative success related to each grade. The grade assigned is a component of student understanding of their individual success or lack thereof. It is attributed to success in the general subject matter without any consideration of the sub-elements that constitute an understanding of the general subject. Clearly said: Since the sub-elements/components of the general subject mathematics were not listed, the student gets a vague picture of his competencies for mathematics. It may even be that the student is competent in certain components of the subject mathematics and less or not at all competent in other components. Therefore, such a grading system neither rewards nor informs about the elements of mathematics about which the student excelled, performed adequately, or barely met the basic standard for a particular grade. This reality does not assist a student to first identify and then resolve discrepancies in his subject knowledge, nor highlight a superior knowledge that might support an accelerated pathway to advanced knowledge, important to the future of the student. The status quo is incomplete in its appraisal of student knowledge, but it currently represents the status quo.

By applying a more competency-based approach, it is possible to engage and motivate a student by informing them of their current status and remaining knowledge necessary to achieve their objectives. Such knowledge will increase student apparent control of their learning experience and simultaneously accelerate and improve the learning process.

Consider again the subject of Mathematics but as a general and, in this case, a targeted Result Area. The objective is to enable the topic to be mastered through the study of its composite areas of knowledge or the "sum of its parts," each measurable against a comprehensive standard and available for introduction into the student pool of knowledge in a fashion and time appropriate to each student.

Reviewing once again the subject of Mathematics [Result Area], let us consider the composite areas of knowledge [Competencies], mastery of which is required to truly understand Mathematics. Referring to the diagram below, we find the Result Area subject to the study of the application of numbers as they relate to quantity, structure, space, and change [Sub-Competencies].

These sub-competencies are generally studied within the following topics, each of which is required at some level and dimension in order to be certified as competent on the subject. Quantity is ordinarily studied through Numbers Theory, Structure is analyzed most frequently through Algebra, Space is analyzed through Geometry, and Change is studied in the realm of Trigonometry and Applied Mathematics. A very robust topic, but expertise is attainable through the step-by-step assessment and approach suggested by the Competency Model.

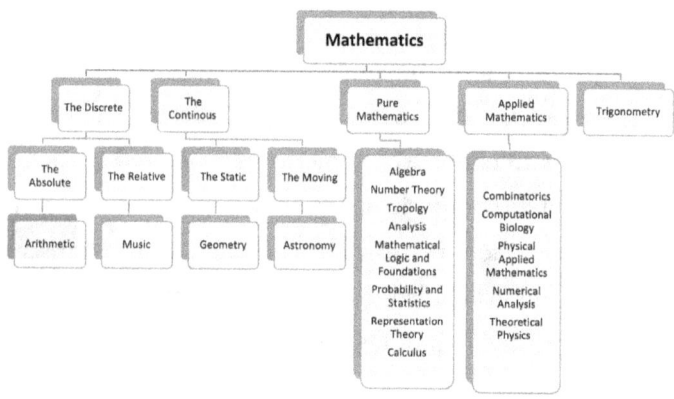

FIGURE 3: Segmentation of Mathematics from an Educational Perspective

The process reveals two distinct opportunities (among others): Disclosure of the level of competency possessed by an individual in each of the sub-competencies and, by consolidation, the level of expertise possessed on the Competency (in this case) Mathematics. Additionally, it establishes for the institution or enterprise the inventory of desirable knowledge [Competencies] resident in their pool of resources currently, and what discrepancies exist in those competencies in support of their future objectives.

The worst-case scenario of the process is the detailed assessment of resources at a much more granular level and the potential disclosure of talent previously unknown to either the institution or the enterprise.

Rethinking the model, consider again the subject of Mathematics as a Result Area composed of expertise classified as sub-competencies. The aggregation of each establishes a true level of expertise developed from the bottom-up rather than trying to assess (or guess) at what possible areas of expertise a candidate may possess (or merely claim). Thus, considering mathematics as an overarching concept of smaller result areas, which in turn are subdivided into competencies and finally into sub-competencies and levels of competence.

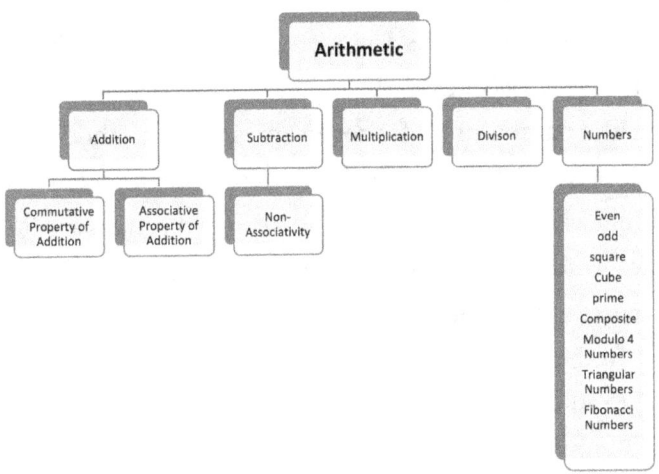

Figure 4: The Sub-Competencies of Arithmetic

This type of granular competency-based learning strategies provides flexibility in the way that course credit may be earned or awarded and provides students with more personalized learning opportunities. Vehicles for adding or enhancing competencies include resident, online, and blended learning processes, dual enrollment as well as the inclusion of advanced credit courses in high schools, project-based and community-based learning, and life credit for experience, to introduce only a few opportunities to expand competency.

This innovative learning environment promotes more student engagement as it focuses content on those aspects most desirable and useful to each student according to their need and resident competencies. This self-directed customization model will promote a more satisfying outcome for both parties and a more cost-effective solution for all parties concerned.

The paradigm under review presents a methodology through which we may act to develop pathways that will ultimately lead to processes and outcomes that disable failed ideas and migrate toward more efficient and productive aspects of the model.

In the end, the methodology must better identify and more fully utilize critical talent resident in and required of a human resource pool.

II. TOWARD A COMPETENCY-BASED APPLICATION FOR ENTERPRISES

Rethinking the Current Model

The process of securing and managing human resources (talent) has changed little over the last generation in traditional business models. The myriad of challenges to these models recently experienced may lead to a rethinking of talent-selection-and-development processes within entity resource pools and, indeed, in markets.

The fallacy perpetuated is that companies look to staff positions and job positions instead of human resources capable of executing desired outcomes—and, potentially, so much more.

Often confronted with budget limitations or abrupt market changes, enterprises must often narrowly focus on the challenge *du jour*, the solution for which is included in a job description without a more effective survey of the business needs beyond. Though this path may give the illusion of cost savings from this immediate solution, it overlooks the potential benefit of selecting human resource talent that is capable of both immediately executing to the desired outcome in the short term *and* introducing value beyond the basic qualifications that resulted in their initial selection. The result, though satisfactory, is absolutely suboptimum, more costly, and potentially catastrophic in the longer term.

How might an entity effectively restructure to achieve this additional benefit? What key elements must be considered in the process? Does the organigram or organizational hierarchy matrix define the enterprise needs fully or serve only to further escalate the process? Is the driving force behind change internal, spearheaded by an enterprise executive change agent, or external, driven by consultants?

The answer to these questions is not always straightforward. A senior executive in the pharmaceutical industry once described both hiring and firing to be kindred concepts; that was an early nod to the GIG concept of talent management. There was a need to fill an immediate fail-point, with little or no consideration given to the future implications of the decision. Once the immediate task is completed and that particular issue no longer exists, the talent hired to resolve the problem is separated from the company, and those costs are no longer a burden to the company. This patchwork process may have continuous and devastating effect on the viability and competitiveness of the company. At its basic core is a lack of corporate culture continuity.

Competency-based analysis has already yielded valuable insight into the most beneficial pathways to educate our children in attaining and improving language skills. The time has come to integrate the most appropriate aspects of these previous studies into business organizations to support the recruitment, selection, retention, and development of talent.

Optimally, this will include a transparency with regard to the integration of all academic and trade competencies throughout the enterprise workforce. The growing interest in competency-based human resource (talent) management mandates a focus on the provision of a common framework, including vocabulary and definitions enabling all motivated participants to speak with a *lingua franca*.

The new model presented in this book makes the attempt to bridge differences in perception to form such a platform that builds upon the initial introduction with homage to the CEFR in the European Union. This should facilitate a faster growth curve both in process acceptance and business results.

Before addressing the "how" to establish a common framework, it is desirable to clarify more thoroughly the "why." Viewing all the various analyses performed on competency-based business performance by numerous organizations, such as TRACE, CEDEFOP, and UNESCO, it is clear that the current state of business operations in general fell short of the desired results.

TRACE has clearly suggested that confronting the challenges of shrinking populations, severe skill shortage, the necessity to train and develop the workforce in the light of rapid changes in work practices and across global markets, there is a growing need for common qualification standards and certification.

WHY BUSINESS PROCESS MANAGEMENT EFFICIENCY IS CRITICAL FOR ENTERPRISES IN ANY INDUSTRY

Standard business processes have already been reviewed and defined by industry groups and are the core of business process flows today. Every organization operates to some degree with a series of steps/processes that enable it to take an order and provide and bill for product or services following the successful delivery of the goods or service. These processes are replicated, constantly being improved and adjusted as disruptions occur and are resolved. The common term describing this phenomenon over the last century is *continuous improvement*. It has become one of the hallmarks of an enterprise exhibiting strong competitive advantage.

These processes are an aggregate of tasks, executed repetitively across time, with resulting flow, whether that be order processing, billing, converting invoices to cash, refreshing the credit line, etc. The major difference between the process and its composite tasks is the fact that process changes in both rate and volume, while tasks represent a single event in a specific time frame, upon which the business relies to maintain the entirety of the business process cycle.

Possible examples include:

Onboarding processes often include new-employee enterprise-introduction briefings. These often introduce the culture of the enterprise, require the signing of a confidentiality agreement, among other internal control documents, introduce immediate management and peers in the intended organization, etc. This process has been refined over time, and experience dictates that the process be delivered each time in the same manner.

Once accepted over time as a priority process, the enterprise introduces the steps as a formal procedure, accompanying enterprise policy upon which the enterprise will rely. These procedures become part of the corporate culture, are memorialized on different media (paper, electronic files and memory, etc.), and become organization SOP (Standard Operating Procedure). In this manner, the enterprise is assured all associates receive the same initial and continuous message on the particular topic.

Part of the continuing challenge to establishing a common framework is the large number of informal processes that exist throughout organizations; through time, they have become accepted practice, although they have never been documented or recognized as an official procedure. This will be one of the many integration challenges in creating a common framework.

Elemental to the processes is the myriad of independent or aggregative tasks that can occur repetitively or as required by the process. One-off collection contacts result in a favorable conclusion and are not repetitive. Tasks that are informal yet occur more regularly may not be required as a permanent part of the business and would not receive documentation or become a permanent enterprise written procedure. For due-diligence purposes, this is often discouraged, but, nevertheless, these are features that must be considered in the formation of a common framework for enterprises.

It is critical to recognize that the efficiency of the business process flow determines the success of the enterprise. Optimum task efficiency per process translates into best possible process flow for each business process.

This benefit reveals itself in several ways:

Optimum Productivity and Profit—both critical success factors (CSF) of business performance results in:

- *Improved associate morale*—By streamlining processes, the company eliminates waste in tasks and stages that impair efficient operation. Associates will commit more time to task and process efficiency and contribute directly to continuous improvement without a direct mandate. This will inevitably lead to greater satisfaction of all parties.
- *Happier customers*—Through fewer defects, faster product- and service-delivery time, and overall perception of delight in customer service, the brand and reputation of the enterprise will grow.

Efficient business process management helps companies leverage their resources in alignment with business objectives, while delivering on customer promises and maximizing agility to react to market demands and new customers. The greater the understanding of what the business processes are, how they function, and what impact they have, the better a business is managed. How well these processes operate can be the differentiator between a *good* organization and a *great* organization.

In order to achieve this success, an initial review and alignment of the business processes is necessary. Business Process Mapping ensures efficient operations driven by the best range of processes, streamlined, cohesive, and effective, with the outcome providing the most value from the enterprise factors of production or service.

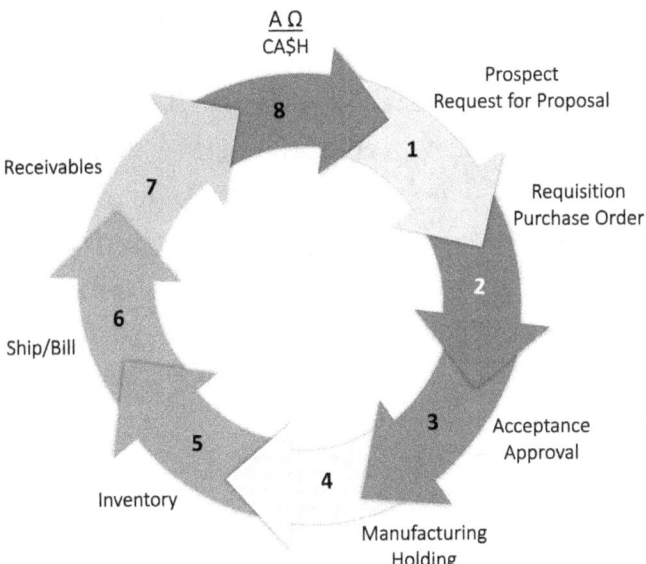

Figure 5: The Business Operating Cycle

For that reason alone, we begin with consideration of the various business processes. Key Result Areas under analysis to form the common framework transcend all enterprises, large or small, manufacturing-, distribution-, or service-oriented. Research has already been introduced into the analysis of business processes. It is at the heart of the Business Process Management (BPM) strategy that identifies desirable steps to effect an optimum solution, driven by scientific methodology. Various other approaches have touched upon the use of Emotional Quotient in order to identify the best customer-management processes and methodologies to create competitive advantage.

Though not executed in a structured way across all Result Areas, the areas of analysis did add somewhat to the improvement of outcome for the enterprise, but the extent of improvement depended upon the level, extent, and commitment of the enterprise. Further, the improvement persisted only so long as the change agent retained his direct interest in driving the process. Introducing competency-based business process integrates itself into the corporate DNA and becomes organic to the enterprise and continuous, without the need for specific direction or even guidance.

WHAT ARE THESE BUSINESS PROCESSES[10]?

As previously discussed, much of business process as described in the order-to-cash cycle is similar and varies mostly according to size of enterprise and investment in operating-system maintenance and upgrades. Our approach will be to investigate the business cycle with the objective to identify a set of Result Areas that are common across all enterprises. We will review these Result Areas within a business-to-business organization. For the most part, business operations are concentrated in four operational areas[11]:

1. Prospect to Order (PTO)
2. Order to Cash (O2C)
3. Supply Chain Management (SCM)
4. Procure to Pay (PTP)

Generally, the scope of these processes spans the entirety of business operations. They convert sales prospects into orders, ultimately into cash. These processes, though similar, are also subject to operating software oversight by SAP, Oracle, etc. Business processes are driven by the business requirements and controls, usually under the oversight of a C-level Executive.

---

10 For a more detailed report on the Business Processes, please see Appendix II.
11 Connelly, *Trade Credit Risk Management*, Third Edition 2017, by approval of the author

These key organizations include:

- Sales
- Product Pricing and Marketing
- Accounting and Finance
- Strategy/Budgeting

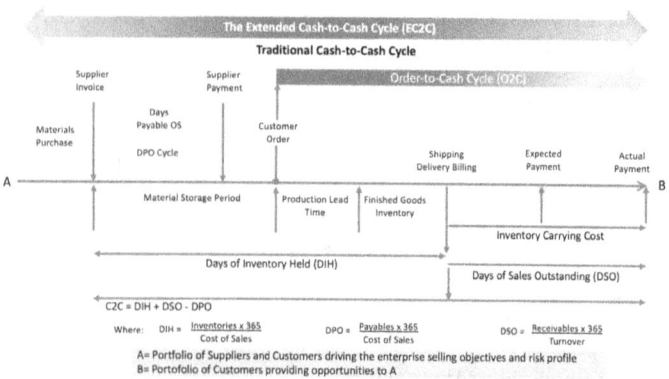

FIGURE 6: The Extended Cash-to-Cash Cycle (EC2C)

STANDARDIZING ORGANIZATION COMPETENCIES

A popular business-performance target, *continuous improvement* refers to the management of business processes in such a way as to improve period-to-period. It relates to the need to constantly survey performance and outcome of business processes to ensure improvement with every passing fiscal period. By identifying potential delays in the business process cycle, organizations ensure both focus and resolution of impediments to strategic and operational objectives.

Ongoing analyses, down to the smallest detail, result in the recognition of potential issues and actual delay events that impair improvement in the business cycle. Solutions result in more efficient and streamlined processes that support a more agile response to any impediment.

Process mapping for improvement or new implementations is greatly enhanced by these process flow improvements.

In a digitized world, software is a facilitator, and the construct of actual or desired behavior takes the form of either flow-chart or workflow-management software, although pencil and paper are also an option.

Consider a typical simple Mapping Process for a baking model:

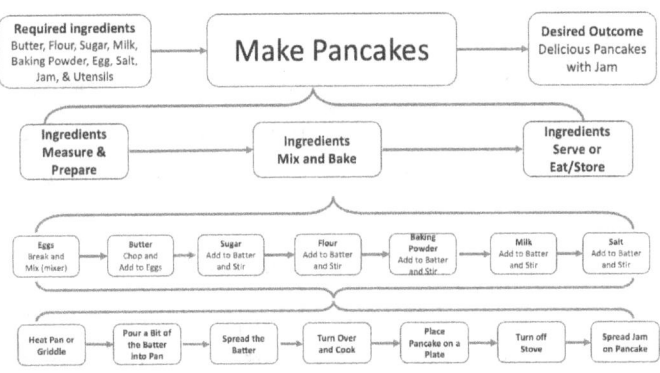

FIGURE 7: A Mapping Process—Making Pancakes

Laying out the process step by step provides an opportunity to establish with clarity and transparency all steps and tasks within each process. Analysts may review and validate each step individually and identify both obvious and concealed shortcomings, redundancies, and features operating at peak efficiency. For purposes of the Competency Paradigm, this enables a clear pathway to view all competencies, sub-competencies, levels, and dimensions that are required to fully understand and manage the processes.

This process does give rise to a certain number of questions. There would be a number of risks that would need to be considered before such a project could begin. They include: Are there steps in the process that are too time consuming? Does the step or task analysis consume more time than you think is appropriate? Is there a way to accelerate such steps and extract more efficiency? Is the process expected to cause missed deadlines or delays?

What could cause these delays? Are certain anticipated process changes more costly than the return would support? What is the risk and source of price increases during the course of the project?

In any process, there are key tasks, the efficiency of which determine the rate, amount, and productivity of the output. Referring back to the previous "Pancake Process," the processes seem rather simple to identify and straightforward. But is this truly the case? If the details are not captured correctly, or quantity measures entered incorrectly, or the steps are executed in a less efficient or outright wrong order, then the previously referenced pancake batter will bake at too high a temperature, leading to a failed overall process.

Is the assigned leadership structured to efficiently execute the process and, as a consequence, establish a flow of responsibility and authority that assures a successful process? Will next-level managers demonstrate experience and knowledge of the process sufficient to select key associates who can guarantee success of the project? Will they rely on selection according to specific and task-based skills? Selection according to these characteristics will almost certainly limit the potential value of the exercise.

Imagine for a moment that each step in the implementation is executed by a single associate. Now compare that feature with the making pancakes analogy above. Consider the third step in the ingredients process, "Sugar—add to batter and stir." In order to execute this step properly, the following skills are required:

- Good calculation skills in order to correctly recognize and understand the units of measurement and to measure correct quantities
- Notions of ingredients and their reaction as part of the mixture
- Analytical ability to determine whether the preparatory work done has been carried out well by colleagues. Have the correct ingredients been used? Does the pre-dough look exactly as it should?

- Technical skills of the confectionery trade, enabling identification of errors and the resulting consequences, along with necessary corrective action.
- Empathy for the composition of the pre-dough and addition of the sugar in the mixing process. Should all the sugar be added at the same time, or should small amounts be added gradually? Does an incomplete or incorrect delivery of the sugar into the mix impact the final outcome of the pancake batter?
- Technical skills to deal with the respective utensil (in this case, the scales and mixer [blender])
- Risk and safety awareness. Comply with safety regulations to avoid injuries. What corrective action or first aid must be taken in the event of an accident?
- Good communication skills to share observations regarding bottlenecks or other emerging situations quickly and effectively with colleagues.
- Innovative thinking, risking a change in the recipe for a possible improved result, a better pancake.

An accomplished pastry chef would admit that the consistency of the pancake batter is determined by the quality of the ingredients and the choice of ingredients: mixed eggs with sugar, or butter with sugar. A less-experienced preparer may simplify the process by delivering all ingredients into one bowl and mix all together at one time. Given the elements of a high-quality product, would that process provide the same end result? This is precisely the point in discussion at which knowledge of a process brings the most value.

It is this simple reflection upon a known process, that of making pancakes, that presents a clear understanding of the actual and potential value of human resources available to any enterprise. Unquestionably, in today's talent-management world, much, if not most, of an associate's skills, knowledge, and experience remain hidden dimensions. These are rendered moot if they are not directly associated with the features of a given job as described in the hiring job description. The extent of loss to enterprises defies quantification.

Thought process has multiple dimensions and may prove ineffective if not sequentially approached. Learning in a step-by-step manner reinforces the learning experience and enables earlier, successful replication of desired behavior.

Some have voiced concern that desired outcomes in business will be achieved only when associates have acquired or developed a broad scope or perspective as it relates to business processes. However, history reflects that much, if not most, talent is selected based upon a specific but limited skill set. This is a practice that is reinforced by job descriptions.

The need for associate support may also result in the selection of a *currently available* resource, as opposed to the most *appropriate* or *effective* resource. Given that stress, it is likely that the selection of an associate with some talent in necessary areas is better than forgoing an immediate hire because associates fail to demonstrate complete presence of desirable traits.

An argument may be made that, in general, managers have neither the time nor the necessary expertise to effectively select talent for their teams. Similarly, it is possible that most managers do not have a broad business process knowledge beyond the area for which they have direct responsibility. Further complication exists when the hiring manager lacks the experience or knowledge necessary to determine exactly which competencies are most impactful or desirable for company objectives, as measured against the traits exhibited by potential new hires.

An effective hiring decision is critical to the smooth functioning of an organization. For example, should the purchasing department require an associate, that person will most likely need to demonstrate an understanding of the purchase process. Similarly, the Human Resources Department will require a basic knowledge of talent management consistent with current practices.

Enterprises today, referring back to our making pancakes analogy, provide a sketchy list of ingredients with some guidance on experience in making pancakes, but the decision remains incomplete and at risk by reason of an incomplete assessment of the breadth and depth of the potential talent. This presents the enterprise with a potentially harmful and costly decision, despite the fact that it was made considering the best talent available, meeting the requirements of the hire.

Simply put, imagine that a human resource hiring associate is supported by a process map outlining the critical areas of knowledge and experience expected of a new hire. Further imagine a next-stage process supplemented by a process map that has been fully mapped out and available to preliminarily scan potential talent that is currently or potentially of value to the enterprise.

Further enhance that model to include a common vocabulary and framework available to enterprise that permits a full comprehension of the pool of talent currently resident in the enterprise—as well as what resources might be interesting for the future development of the enterprise. The competency model represents that vehicle.

At a granular level, most associates are likely to understand the necessary outcome. That enables more open-minded and effective communication supporting innovative thinking of both challenges and opportunities to the enterprise. Restructuring the previous model for "**Making Pancakes**," the process has now been divided into Result Areas and competencies (see above). Designed to move forward as business condition and employee motivation permit, the competency-based approach introduces its value-add in an opportune and noninvasive way.

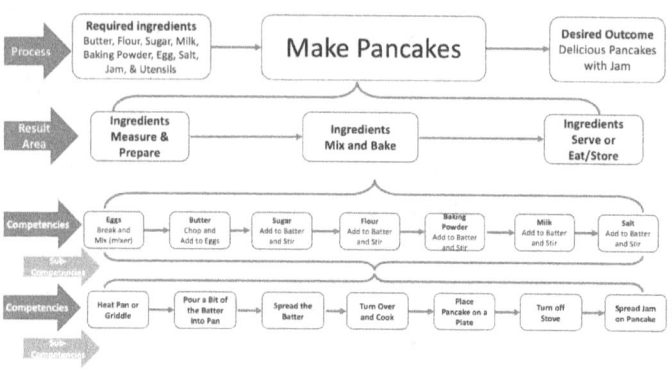

Figure 8: Complete Mapping Process—Making Pancakes

Basically, it provides the opportunity for a potential associate to fully understand the discrete competencies required and introduce previously dormant competencies of potential value to the hiring enterprise.

CREATE A COMMON DICTIONARY OF COMPETENCIES AND SUB-COMPETENCIES

All enterprises in all markets are currently wrestling with fiscal and economic challenges that require a wider focus and a broader, stronger, and more sustained individual and collective performance, perhaps in areas not currently within the brevet or task assignment of associates.

Turnover both voluntary and involuntary is perennially a problem in organizations. The resource whose services are secured at significant expense for a specific function as directed by a job description is generally evaluated on factors that fulfill the basic requirements of the job. As business conditions change, the associate may, in short order, experience elimination due to a change in market conditions or voluntarily sever the relationship due to lack of satisfaction in the job secured or further opportunity. Without a pathway for further achievement, the more desirable associates depart, utilizing the skills and experience your enterprise has provided in the interest, possibly, of your competitor.

But, also important—perhaps *more* important—will be the process such as suggested to widen the search to identify current competencies within all segments of the enterprise to create a universal enterprise resource pool that will identify desirable and even critical competencies resident in associates who remain under-utilized or not utilized in the best interest of the enterprise. The proposed programs focus attention on **competencies** resident within the enterprise, identify sub-competency gaps within competencies particularly desirable to companies, and enable enterprises of all sizes and venues to plan in a more economically efficient manner. By better managing these resources, it is possible to reduce inefficient hiring and termination practices, reduce the loss of corporate memory that enables faster productivity schedules, and applies scarce expense resources in a much more productive manner.

A NEW COMPETENCY-BASED PROCESS

Program implementation, in effect, is a search and a solution to the identification of competencies, resident and known, resident and unknown, and desirable but not yet resident. Strategic plans take on a dimension previously unknown that may commit, in advance, human capital resources necessary to optimize the potential for a successful fiscal period. Success here will be driven by the ability to optimize existing talent through more complete utilization and further development of competencies currently recognized in the traditional manner.

Experience has demonstrated that the value of competency, even in its most basic form, will be recognized immediately by all industry group professionals, and in both the basic and advanced form as a key driver of both top- and bottom-line performance for their respective enterprises. Basic competency implies the ability to execute a task or series of tasks in an acceptable fashion. This level of performance has been the historical basis of employment retention.

In order to discuss the New Competency model, it is necessary to produce standardized definitions through which to communicate easily and effectively. Therefore, the Order-to-Cash Cycle is a particularly beneficial starting point for such investigation, defined first by the domain bounded from "point-of-order" to "cash conversion" of the invoice. It is also referred to as O2C or OTC, or the Invoice to Cash Cycle; it belongs to the heartbeat processes and is the most critical and complex one of any organization.

It is the process supporting maximum profitable selling and customer-portfolio development and is one of the most outsourced business processes. The value to the enterprise is most obvious and provides a solid return on investment . . . a good place to begin.

TYPICAL RESULT AREAS OF THE O2C BUSINESS PROCESS

The Order to Cash Cycle represents the entire group of processes from order entry to cash application, often referred to generally as the Order-to-Cash Cycle (OTC or O2C) and is specifically divided into the Order-to-Invoice (OTI) and Invoice-to-Cash (ITC) cycles. Enterprise industry groups with operational expertise have defined eight operational areas—**Result Areas** (RA)—included in these cycles. This expertise forms the basis for the creation of a common group of RA that will form the group of General Accepted Result Areas (GARA). In research, the process descriptions of Boston Consulting Group (BCG)[13] best align with the broadest scope and our objectives.

In its simplest and most basic form, the process enables better and more productive utilization of existing resources and better management of people. As one of the most critical business process flows, we begin with a discussion of the structure used to establish a general competency matrix throughout the Order-to-Cash Cycle [O2C]. In order to identify the most desirable [and critical] competencies, we first deconstruct the O2C business cycle into the following processes, henceforth referred to as **Result Areas**:

- Order Management
- Credit Management
- Order Fulfillment and Returns
- Order Shipping (Pick and Pack)
- Customer Invoicing
- Accounts Receivable
- Cash Application
- Dispute Management
- Reporting and Data Management

These Result Areas, generally already in place in most organizations in one form or another, provide a basis to measure current efficiency and comparative results of the change in performance. The standardization of competencies and required definitions as developed and applied to each Result Area enable the program to overcome normal project inertia and accelerate outcomes.

Building upon the CEFR process, major Result Areas are further deconstructed one step into operational components, known as Competencies. These enable businesses to specify or confirm each element deemed critical to business functionality. The Competencies allow a business a more granular look to its process; compare it with the Make Pancakes Process. A baseline description of the competencies and sub-competencies is included in the new model. The more effectively competencies are introduced and applied to the process, the more efficient the operations and more productive the outcome.

For the sake of simplicity and understanding of this complex subject, we further describe each of the Result Areas in order to determine first the desirable competencies and then the composite sub-competencies necessary to present a complete resource competency. These are the summaries of executable task/steps that employees or prospect candidates must be able to do in a competent manner to be able to say that he can fulfill the objective of the Result Area.

To that end, it should be shared that, as with CEFR general Result Areas and competencies, these are naturally subject to the business environment in which they are to be applied, and further standardization would be adjusted as the model is implemented and integrated into enterprise business process.

The business-process flow provides good structure through which to discuss the development of the most desirable enterprise competency pool. As going concerns, these Result Areas will currently exist in most enterprises. They form the basis through which trade is accomplished and results are commonly [and presumably] measured and reported. Ultimately, all these competencies have largely been agreed on.

To begin a comprehensive understanding of the new model, let us consider a single Result Area as a first step in understanding the larger and more complicated process of optimizing associate value. The O2C cycle is further defined as follows:

It is determined that the first Result Area, "Order Management," requires, at a minimum, the following *competencies*:

- Master data collection
- Verification and storage
- Customer creation
- Multichannel management
- Receiving, validating, and entering orders
- System/software savvy

A business requires at least the following *competencies* in the second Result Area, "Credit Management":

- Customer portfolio
- Credit risk assessment and monitoring
- Credit limit and payment term
- Credit trade risk instruments
- Financial analysis
- Sales contract review (long-term or short-term)

- GTC (General Terms and Conditions) review
- System/software savvy

A business requires at least the following *competencies* in the third Result Area, "Order Fulfillment and Returns":

- Product availability
- Order and return confirmation
- Delivery tracking
- System/software savvy

A business requires at least the following *competencies* in the fourth Result Area, "Order Shipping":

- Product Pick and Pack
- Shipping goods
- Return Merchandize Authorization (RMA) management
- System/software savvy

A business requires at least the following *competencies* in the fifth Result Area, "Customer Invoicing."

- Billing management (manual, digital)
- E-billing
- Calculation
- Verification
- Reporting

- System/software savvy

A business requires at least the following *competencies* in the sixth Result Area, "Accounts Receivable."

- Collection strategy
- Cash management and generation
- Forecasting and reporting
- Dunning process
- Bad debt and write-off
- System/software savvy

A business requires at least the following *competencies* in the seventh Result Area, "Cash Application (Account Reconciliations)."

- Cash posting
- Unallocated cash management
- Bank and account reconciliations
- Bank systems/credit cards
- Payment methods
- Discrepancies resolution
- System/software savvy

A business requires at least the following *competencies* in the eighth Result Area, "Dispute Management."

- Dispute identification
- Third-party complaint resolution
- Credit-notes processing
- Root-cause eradication
- Lean management analysis
- System/software savvy

A business requires at least the following *competencies* in the ninth Result Area, "Reporting and Data Management."

- Gather, validate, and report on data management
- Data-security guidelines
- C-Suite-level reports (dashboard)
- Forecast calculations
- System/software savvy
- KPI reports:
  - Aging Trial Balance (ATB)
  - Probability of Default (POD)
  - Days Sales Outstanding (DSO)
  - Average Days Delinquent (ADD) Report
  - Incoming/outstanding cash and sales ratio

We believe that there will be very little criticism among Order-to-Cash professionals regarding the appropriateness of the competencies as defined in this book. The list of competencies is quite incomplete.

It is the objective of this book to introduce new dimensions of identifying, reinforcing, and optimally recognizing and utilizing human resource talent in the best possible interest of the enterprise. A challenge will only improve the substance and outcome of the new model.

THE DIVISION OF COMPETENCIES INTO SUB-COMPETENCIES OF THE O2C BUSINESS PROCESS

If a competency was so clear and so short and so concise, businesses would not need excerpts of competencies. But the reality is that competencies are very complex. In order to better enable their functionality and usability, we propose to divide these competencies into smaller competency groups by breaking them into subgroups that make them less complex and more logical and accessible. The breakdown of the Result Areas in Competencies is the first step in understanding the complexity of such a process.

The further dissection of the competencies into their attributed sub-competencies brings more clarity and transparency and a narrower approach in what is expected from an employee or prospect candidate. This granularity is the stage in which a company gains a thorough insight into the individual gears that run the process. Remember, for example, the competency "adding sugar to the batter" in the "Make Pancakes" process.

There are several sub-competencies required that will make this step in the process a success. If these sub-competencies are ignored, it can jeopardize the consistency of the batter and ultimately the pancake. It is the same with the example of the business process O2C cycle. Each of the dozen or so competencies deemed critical to success and the creation of opportunity must be broken down into four sub-competencies.

These four sub-competencies are technical, functional, operational, and behavioral elements. These four dimensions offer a very detailed way to analyze, evaluate, and, if necessary, train a person's level of competence at a 360-degree level. A more thorough look into these dimensions will elaborate their selection.

THE FUNCTIONAL DIMENSION OF SUB-COMPETENCY ANALYSIS—THE "WHAT"

The functional dimension introduces the need for sub-competency focus on specifics that enable the execution of the competency that results in successful Result Area performance. The word "functional" comes from the Latin word *functio*, meaning "performance." It can also describe whether something is working properly. In the current environment that is job-description based, both the requisitioning organization and the enterprise Human Resources group determine what the most desirable characteristics are and which candidates satisfy those needs.

The focus is typically on a broader application, such as communication, listening, command of the written word, interpersonal interaction, computer skills, basic mathematics, and general integrity. Functional competency is characterized by a specific knowledge, skill, or experience that contributes to the potential for success of the person being considered for a challenge.

A functional competency is a specific knowledge or skill area that relates to successful performance in the job. The term "functional," as used in education, indicates application of knowledge that is concrete and usable rather than abstract and theoretical. This means that the aspect of the term has its roots in academia, where having functional knowledge often refers to a body of knowledge that is execution oriented, much like a trade, which requires an internship and journeymanship completion before a person can be certified competent.

Functional skills are the essential knowledge, skills, and understanding that an individual needs in order to operate confidently, effectively, and independently in life and work. In a professional environment, the functional elements of a job an employee is hired to do are the most important components of his function in the company. In many traditions, business process is an amalgam of both aspects of the term, each providing reinforcement and contributing to the successful outcome of these very real-world, essentially non-academic processes.

Functional skills are competencies that are transferable to many different work settings and are specific and measurable in positive qualities of any outcome. It is imperative that the employee understands how, when, and where he or she can use and apply functional sub-competencies.

In the case of Result Area 7 above, that of Cash Application (Account Reconciliations) and its third competency "Bank and Account Reconciliations," a key functional sub-competency presents itself in the form of the need to . . .

"Prepare a bank reconciliation statement; analyze, detect and clarify any discrepancies between the accounting records of the entity and the bank; report the findings and provide solutions to avoid discrepancies in the future."

The practical objective of this exercise is to reduce or eliminate discrepancies.

The classic description of this sub-competency often includes terms with action tones, including: "prepare, analyze, detect, clarify, report, and provide." The objective is active resolution beyond task and process analysis. "Functional" generally implies an active business response in the enterprise world and should indicate the **functional** experience and knowledge expected of the employee or prospect candidate.

THE TECHNICAL DIMENSION OF SUB-COMPETENCY ANALYSIS—THE "HOW"

The word "technology" or "science of craft" comes from the Greek τέχνη, *techne*—"art, skill, cunning of hand"—and λογία, *logia*—is the sum of techniques, skills, methods, and processes used in the production of goods or services or in the accomplishment of objectives. Solid competency means command of and proficiency in using technical resources necessary to effect a satisfactory solution. Therefore, technical skills refer to the knowledge and expertise needed to accomplish complex actions, tasks, and processes; having these skills assumes proficiency in the tasks needed for a specific job.

Technical skills are the practical abilities and knowledge needed to perform specific tasks—often mechanical, information-technology, mathematical, or scientific tasks. These might take the form of mechanical- or industrial-engineering knowledge, command of mathematics, or various aspects of science or technology suitable to supplement other sub-competencies in forming a comprehensive [and competitive] competency. Practical examples include expertise in understanding and coding high-demand programming languages, design programs, mechanical equipment, and tools.

Technical skills are often required to operate machinery, tools, software, and coding, a mastery of which can translate to technically skilled employees or prospect candidates being more confident when applying to certain industries. These are the easiest skills to teach because it takes repeated teaching/training until the student or employee masters the technology. In today's markets, these sub-competencies are often desirable in areas of logistics and transportation, as well as design of infrastructures in enterprises that are involved with the entire business cycle.

Knowledge in these areas often translates into additional sub-competency in the analysis of complex systems. Mastering the technology helps employees to work more efficiently, boosts their confidence, and makes them more valuable candidates for employers. Technical competence describes specialized knowledge the employee has and the ability to apply methods and theoretical knowledge to a specific, individual case. Often enterprise continuity and succession plans seek input from associates with these key sub-competencies, creating important opportunities. Therefore, it is considered one of three key competencies ("skills") necessary as prerequisites for successfully fulfilling management functions.

Reflecting back on our example for the O2C business process in Result Area 7 above, that of Cash Application (Account Reconciliations) and its third Competency "Bank and Account Reconciliations," this additional sub-competency might take the form of a capability to "Read and understand a bank statement, its abbreviations, and terminology; use mathematics to understand the difference between transactions, depositing, and withdrawing funds; recommend enhancement as part of global digitalization and increased efficiency."

Descriptions in this sub-competency should reflect the technical contribution to the overall competency objective of the Result Area—such as "read, understand, use, recommend"—and should indicate the **technical** experience and knowledge expected of the employee or prospect candidate.

THE OPERATIONAL DIMENSION OF SUB-COMPETENCY ANALYSIS—THE "WHICH"

Operational means "immediately effective," "concerning certain measures" (Latin *operari*, "expend labor on"). Operational ability arises when actions can be mastered and carried out fluently, usually achievable only through practical action. Operational ability is characteristically associated with the abilities to think analytically, execute lateral thinking, act objectively under conflicting scenarios, communicate effectively, and execute effectively.

Described differently, an operational parameter represents the bound attributed to a given process or responsibility. Further, an operational definition generally describes the elements of a process leading to an *understanding of the process* rather than a theoretical definition *describing a process*. In other words, an operational definition is generally understood to describe the steps of assigning empirically detectable, observable, or inquired indicators to a theoretical term.

More specifically, theoretically, "credit" is the sale of goods or services on faith, in return for the promise of payment of a given value at some defined future point in time. An operational definition would describe a transaction wherein I give product to you without immediate payment and expect you to pay the debt in thirty days from today. The result is a period wherein credit has been granted, enabling you to depart with the goods you require and, hopefully, sell the goods at a profit in order to repay me and purchase additional goods. It is the statement of procedures used in defining the terms of a process and in determining the existence of a product or service and its properties.

With respect to the new model, sub-competency definitions in this area should reflect their application to the business process—for example, in describing assignment of empirically detectable, observable indicators to a theoretical term, or the statement of procedures used in defining of a process of determining available resource or demand for a product or service and its relevant properties. The procedures included in definitions should be repeatable and comprehensible by anyone and able to be initiated and carried out by everyone.

A key objective of the operational sub-competency is to assure a process definition that can be readily duplicated with minimum difficulty by a general population. Refer again to Result Area 7, above, Cash Application (Account Reconciliations) and its third competency, "Bank and Account Reconciliations," and the manner in which it relates to the Operational sub-competency. In discussing boundaries and/or conditions that represent operational parameters within which a system is designed to function, an operational definition of this sub-competency might include *"Operational ability to recognize the nuances from the different banks of displaying transactions, deposits, and withdrawals; adhere to the operational parameters, such as policies and regulations designed by the bank and company; recommend lean and security methods to simplify the adherence to operational parameters, and increase operational and security effectiveness."*

Descriptions for this dimension of the sub-competency should reinforce actions in process methodology such as "recognize, adhere, or recommend," reflecting operational analysis and influence that indicates the **operational** experience and knowledge expected of the employee or prospect candidate.

THE BEHAVIORAL DIMENSION OF SUB-COMPETENCY ANALYSIS—THE "WHY"

During the course of sub-competency introduction, one of the most difficult aspects to assess is that of behavior. Despite that fact, a behavioral sub-competency is one of the most desirable of them all. Behavioral skills are the most non-identifiable and the most demanded by employers. Assessing competency in a given Result Area often takes the form of behavior evaluation in the midst of execution. Therefore, in this book, we will look at "behavior" from the intrinsic aspect with the question, "Why would I do, or want, or decide something?"

In most competency models, proficiency in an indicated competency is demonstrated through behaviors, which leaves us with questions, such as: What are the skills that are truly being manifested in the behavior? Will such behavior be repeated consistently under various conditions of stress, or will there occur a modification—for better or worse—under different circumstances? Is this a consistently manifested behavior by the person, or is it a mimicked behavior from a more successful colleague? Therefore, it begs the question of why individuals act the way they do under the conditions noted at the time. If someone is mimicking another's behavior without understanding the underlying skill, it will most likely not lead to similar results.

These are particularly important questions to have answered if the associate in question is listed in a succession plan or on a promotion list, or is in a position to influence people by their behavior.

Research on various influencers of behavior for given types of individuals assists in the process of ferreting out risky individuals who might not perform well under general conditions or selecting out individuals who demonstrate poise under great stress and extend that confidence to others as well.

However, for enterprise purposes, it is practical to discuss with the employee a relevant event in which they were challenged. For *Star Trek* fans, a typical operational indicator of behavior might include the following.

At Star Fleet Academy, a key military academic institute, each student is required to face the Kobayashi Maru challenge. Given to every potential officer, it presents a condition wherein the person is confronted with a serious and potentially lethal challenge. As officer in charge, the individual is expected to make as many attempts to defend the ship and crew as possible. Yet all attempts inevitably fail. The reality of the test is that there is *no* outcome that will result in a successful defense. All will die.

The test is meant to measure how the person in charge will face death and lead the crew accordingly. Happily, most business decisions will not be so poorly rewarded, but the point is well made: Character and behavior are generally subject to our historical experiences and the challenges for which we are prepared.

The ability to measure behavioral tendencies, generally through observation, is an important influencer in the determination of this sub-competency and a critical component of a completely competent employee. To bypass these questions and doubts, we add the behavioral attribute as a stand-alone component that can be assessed at proficiency level against the specific sub-competency. We purposely have added "behavioral" as a stand-alone "dimension," in contrast to previous competence models, wherein proficiency is measured with behavioral factors. Observing or assessing behavior as a stand-alone dimension, we can see the truly manifested and intrinsically desired behavior.

Behavioral skills refer to the reflective ability of the individual in relation to the characteristics of the situations he may come up against. We may improve our capacity to render a preliminary opinion on the probable outcome for a given employee by classifying human behavior into four basic personality types: optimistic, pessimistic, trusting, and envious. Seeing behavior through these lenses may help in explaining current behavior and predicting future behavior. Additional granularity is contributed by studies that suggest that there are three fundamental types of behavior:

1. purely practical
2. theoretical-practical
3. purely theoretical

Further insight can be gained by boiling reasons for specific behaviors down to three:

A. a determining reason
B. a motivating reason
C. a supporting reason

Combining both, the result is a table with infinite possibilities, which this book will not consider. The number of studies expands daily, but consideration of this level of detail on the subject is beyond the scope of this book. The aim of this book is to offer employers and recruiters a new method that better illustrates the behavioral skills of their employees and potential candidates.

Continuing on our example for the O2C business process:

- Result Area "Cash Application (Account Reconciliations)"
  - the third competency "Bank and Account Reconciliations"
    - one of the "behavioral" sub-competencies can be "*When performing any form of reconciliation, adhere to standards, values, and rules of conduct associated with one's position and the culture in which one operates. Avoid corrupting factors, and show high integrity in passing on information consistently and honestly, guarding sensitive information.*"

The adjectives and adverbs used in this example, such as "honestly," "incorruptible," and "showing high integrity" should indicate the **behavioral** experience and knowledge expected of the employee or prospect candidate. It is the best way to show expectations of acceptable behavior in the process of confirming this sub-competency.

Depending on the size of the business, these sub-competencies will be nuanced or customized to the business, although in general, the dimensions "technical, functional, operational, and behavioral" will not change.

THE FINAL SEGMENTATION INTO BUILDING BLOCKS

Why is this granularity needed? These granular building blocks provide a systematic methodology, as shown under Appendix II, for allowing a narrowly focused and concrete, targeted learning and assessment goal, similar to the CEFR for languages (Appendix !). Assessing process proficiency (individual) or efficiency (process), the outcome is classified into four levels of proficiency:

- Limited proficiency
- Developing proficiency
- Proficient
- Highly Proficient

We hire and recruit people based on a position but have no knowledge or understanding about the underlying motivation, attitudes, or true skills, thus, the competencies remain hidden. Bringing the competencies to the surface in this form of granular building blocks "attributed sub-competencies" per proficiency level, each granular block fits within a maximum 10-minute range of analysis, testing, learning, and training available in short and independent bursts. Imagine the ease in acquiring a complete competency by its granular building block within a maximum 10-minute range per block.

How does such a granular block look?

For this example, we continue with the Business Process "O2C cycle" and

- the Result Area "Cash Application (Account Reconciliations)" with one of its
  - competencies, "Bank and Account Reconciliation" and its
    - Sub-Competency, Technical "Read and understand bank statements" with its full definition: *"Read and understand a bank statement, its abbreviations and terminology; use mathematics to understand the difference between transactions, depositing, and withdrawing funds; recommend enhancement as part of global digitalization and increased efficiency,"* defining its granular building blocks, such as:
    - Limited proficiency: *"Read and become familiar with a bank statement, its abbreviations, and terminologies."*
    - Developing proficiency: *"Understand a bank statement, its abbreviations, and*

> *terminologies; use accounting skills to distinguish between transactions, deposits, and withdrawals."*
> - Proficient: *"Master the understanding, application, and execution of all transactions, deposits, and withdrawals."*
> - Highly Proficient: *"Provide complete explanation and training materials for understanding all transactions, deposits, and withdrawals, suggesting enhancements as part of change."*

We can use this example to illustrate the simplicity of such a building block. Our research shows that nearly 99% of all organizations that have a "Cash Application/Treasury" department have already created and documented such a work procedure and training. Although an employer or recruiter expects such a technical competency as a prerequisite for an open position in a "Cash Application" team, the organization still arranges an introductory training course during the onboarding procedure of an employee, first to test the existing competence and secondly to train this competence, if not available in employee's competency repertoire.

If we were to set a processing time of 60 minutes only for the creation of work procedures and training plan around this sub-competency, and then extrapolate this to the hourly wage of the respective employee for all organizations requiring such a training, then we would have an exorbitant number of expenses.

These expenses are individually and willingly spent by organizations all over the world in the name of training and talent development, which are then—through "creative accounting"—usually not directly visible but clearly noticeable in the reduced profit margin. A commonly defined competency framework or Generally Accepted Competency Framework per Business Process eliminates this recurring expense.

Interviewing a former senior finance executive for a major tech company, now in his early 70s, showed his view of how businesses have been and still are managed today. "If you are a CFO and you have oversight of a finance organization, you are strategically planning for the next quarter and fiscal year and projecting out the course for the next three years. It is an unfortunate consequence that, though functions are staffed, it is likely that much of the desirable talent required, in the strategic sense, remains a potential local, silent-but-unrecognized value.

Only occasionally, when I recognized particular talent and competency that was underutilized, did I execute a strategy to determine succession possibilities for better utilization of that talent. In this organization of some 350 associates, less than 1% of the talent was identified in this manner. Business functioned through job functions, and associates were secured through resume searches and vetting by Human Resources in our organization. The comfort, then, arose from the knowledge that associates were selected under known standards, trained under known programs, and evaluated periodically to assure constant quality.

Even senior management and executive-level associates were arbitrarily evaluated by cognizant next-level executives. The objective was to maintain the performance consistent with company directives and respond immediately to challenges to that objective. As Senior Vice President, Global Risk Management, I understood to a level of great detail how my Vice Presidents executed their brevet and what the performance outcome contributed to the organizational and enterprise objectives. I knew less well, mostly by briefing, the performance of directors and relied upon the directors to properly manage and develop supervisors and line associates according to enterprise development strategy.

During the construct of this model, it became clear what tremendous values could be secured by characterizing and classifying the competencies and directing them to tasks required by any enterprise. This would pare down talent pools to a core of fiduciarily necessary staff, but enable an enterprise to select from a pool, not necessarily limited to the internal associate pool, in order to effect the solution to a task which, upon completion, would require the enterprise to return the competent person from whence they were sourced.

Certainly, a transition period would be required in implementation, but that is consistent with any change in corporate direction. However, certain consolidations generate real value more immediately than others. In this case, specific competencies could first be assessed within the pool of current associates, anywhere in the enterprise sphere of influence. Then, an external search could remedy a gap task that was not solvable through internal resources.

These resources would be a liability to the enterprise only during the period of contract and would leave behind a process improvement along with the final solution—multiple values from a single source. The most efficient access to this potential is through a common competency framework, supported by the UN or other recognized world entity. Here the question becomes more difficult: Will industry leaders, in this case, O2C professionals, agree to definitions and vocabulary for *one* common set of principles that enable the creation of a single **library of building blocks** for each business process accessible to *everyone*? The library would be a database where all granular building blocks are tagged with name and barcode per business process.

The execution of these steps will enable an enterprise to systematically review processes, coordinate their requirements [competencies] with human resources, and move forward to secure the necessary talent to assure alignment and optimized outcome. Once completed and "**generally**

agreed," they should enable a more fluent and informative business operation, drastically reduce expense, and assure a strong competitive advantage for the enterprise.

For example, in the case of associate recruitment and hiring, the employer or recruiter selects from the building block library those competencies it requires for the work to be accomplished. The building blocks may then be tagged with a title and attached to a position if required. The selection is purely work related and focused on the need of the specific organization. A related benefit results from the marginalizing of common areas of business conflict, such as gender, age, religion, etc. Competency becomes the prime directive and, for future candidates, a pathway to suitability for their career.

Simultaneously advancing both human and process resources will yield faster results in a lower-risk and controlled environment. This system promotes organization competitive advantage through the release of the individual competency constraints of current systems and:

1. fosters individual development with flexibility
2. provides organizations with current inventory of competencies (recognized and utilized, under- or unutilized, and available)
3. enables a strategic view of capacity and need organizationally
4. measures achievement at required levels of operation

5. identifies capacity gaps according to organizational needs (current and projected)
6. identifies training and support needs to fulfill enterprise destiny
7. aligns the corporate culture with its business strategy

Outside of the business world, this model allows vocational and educational institutions to tap into this broad library of granular building blocks and use it effectively in their training and educational programs. This method sets the ground to bridge the gap between vocational/educational training and professional business life.

Therefore, the critical question remains: "Are business leaders ready to agree on one, single common ground of Competency-Based Business Management and support integration of competencies derived from Vocational/Educational Training?"

A properly positioned associate delivers immediate and continuing value and success beyond the scope of the immediate assignment. The enterprise would know from the first hire where that associate fits into the succession plan and would be able to integrate the full range of competencies into the strategic plan for the enterprise.

This same methodology is applicable to all industries, including hospitality, tourism, healthcare, construction, etc., and all institutions worldwide. As a solution, it has merely to be designed to be scalable, for it is, at its core, agile.

Chapter V

GIVEN THE STATUS QUO—A QUANTUM LEAP

As *competency-paradigm description has evolved* and this book's chapters have progressed, the content has become more granular. To that end, this chapter intends to present:

1. Short review of the current state of talent management
2. Typical solutions to the current situation
3. Presentation of the New Model in visual terms
4. Differentiated definition of the New Model.
5. Contra-arguments to the model.
6. Model benefits
    a. A common language spanning employees, educational institutions, business, and government
    b. Focus on the central needs of the organization
    c. Efficient integration of education into enterprises
    d. Integration of AI and other learning IT enhancements into the paradigm
    e. Preparation for a more ad hoc, agile, and GIG-focused world

7. Implications of model adoption
    a. Model construct promotes scalability
    b. Organizations can manage to competency gaps and hire to fill them
    c. Job descriptions simply flow from the model
    d. Enables a "GIG" focus internally and externally
    e. Managers may use the model for directing and assessing internal/external GIG workers

THE CURRENT STATE OF PLAY

We have discussed the fractured nature of the current labor market as well as the responses of the various actors to a broken process. No one is happy with how it functions, nor can we be sure about outcomes. The existing process has many workarounds and patches designed to make it function, and they are, as often as not, designed simply to make the statistical performance of the process better. It does function reasonably well in the task of matching people to roles, at least most of the time. Most of us have long since accommodated to all its inequities and intricacies, so much so that its byzantine nature is hardly noticeable on a daily basis. In fact, entire industries have arisen to help businesses navigate the time and complexity. Even a newer entrant like Indeed.com purports to use its AI to provide the perfect candidates for a given role. But that role depends on an inexact process, and the candidate is judged via automated intelligent resume screening. The results may be better and cheaper than before but will never be able to lead us to the promised land. We are aimed at the wrong target. In fact, we arguably have no target at all.

From a labor-development perspective, our organizations are most often functionally driven: Our recruiting, training, and retention resources are largely divided with an eye to the various functional groups within the enterprise. This applies to the certifications we seek and the development that we provide. This is, to a certain extent, necessary for us to do, as often the functional knowledge is difficult to come by. But it is not sufficient. Organizations do not generate value as individual functions; rather, they generate value via processes that deliver value that the customer will willingly fund.

SOLUTIONS PROPOSED

The evolution of employee development from Scientific Management to Systems Management and more recently, Talent Management, has been driven broadly by an increasing recognition of the necessity of improved productivity and willful engagement of people in the success of the business.

Scientific Management and its successor, Systems Management, were driven by the aspirations of the business for greater output. They drove significant gains in productivity and reduced costs. But they left the person feeling like a cog in a great machine, with little connection to the underlying enterprise or its purpose. This aspirational gap was stark, and businesses sought to address it in a number of ways, especially for those involved in product and process quality.

The newest solution is Talent Management, which arrived in the late 1990s and gained momentum as the millennium unfolded. Talent Management looks at the "life cycle" of the employee-development process from attraction to recruitment, to hiring, and then to retention. Most Talent Management practitioners take an 80/20 approach to this process and focus development on the 20 percent or so who are deemed "high performing/high potential" employees. The underlying premise is that it is too expensive and complicated to develop everyone, so 80% of the talent pool is largely ignored so that the resources may be focused on those most likely to rise in the organization.

Retention activities are likewise focused on this group. This fit well with the Jack Welch GE model of "up or out" that was prevalent as Talent Management arose. The process further isolates those people still desirous of development and improvement but who are overlooked. This lack of "self-actualization," as the psychologists might frame it, can be organizationally devastating especially when experienced by such a large group. While not everyone is "high performance/high potential," nearly everyone may be developed to better serve the needs of customers and to develop areas of interest not directly associated with a person's current role and to satisfy their own aspirational desires.

The Talent Management process lets a large portion of an organization lie fallow. In fact, many organizations go to great lengths not to mention and, in fact, disguise, the 80/20 nature of Talent Management to their employees for morale reasons. The costs to the organization for these choices are immense and include unnecessary legal expenses with disgruntled people, governmental scrutiny, reduced productivity, a degraded customer experience, and lower morale. Talent Management, therefore, struggles to provide the very results that it seeks because, while its conclusions have some merit, its underlying premise is wrong. All employees need to be developed, and all people want to feel "developable."

The current state of things does not prepare an organization for what is arriving at its doorstep at breakneck speed. The Covid pandemic and the global economy's response to it have shown that many previously perceived barriers are not barriers at all. It has also shown that some overlooked items—like water-cooler conversations and face-to-face collaboration—are more necessary than we imagined. The pandemic will prove to be the watershed moment in history that previous pandemics have been.

Furthermore, the GIG economy is arriving at a rapid pace. Labor can be bought and sold on an ad-hoc basis, and all employers will be under increasing pressure to use this market seamlessly with their internal labor. This will fundamentally restructure what a "job" is and ask us to reflect anew on the meaning of "full-time employee" or the exact nature of our relationship to companies and employment. Training is being placed online, and distance learning is seeing content granularized and costs falling rapidly.

Our storied learning institutions are offering distance learning at a fraction of previous on-site cost levels. This calls into question the underlying rationale for educational institutions of every type. There is great ferment within education. The previous trends were unsustainable. Educational costs in the developed world have been rising at rates of many multiples of inflation for 30 years. There will be great change over the next decade.

The former constraints of time, place, and simultaneity are being lifted. We can learn, work, and develop with lessened geographical or time-based impact. We can work as a team, learn, and function within a process without the requirement for simultaneity with other people. These tasks can be performed asynchronously. We are confronted with a world where we can choose to structure with fewer constraints than ever before. Will our labor process remain unchanged in the face of all this? Of course not.

It is past time for simple adaptation or step-by-step evolution. It is time to fundamentally rethink it. Our current methods for hiring and retaining employees do not work, are not scalable, and cannot link to what is coming. It is certain that change is coming, and it is time for us to make some decisions on what that change will be.

THE NEW MODEL

Business functions such as marketing, finance, operations, etc. have traditionally been the building blocks of enterprises. There were many reasons for this, chief among them the need to aggregate knowledge and tasks within self-educating groups. This underlying premise has been supplanted by the ubiquity of information, the technology to link processes, and the realization that change is possible.

Our suggestion is to use organizational functions for strategic organizational development but to use the most basic elements of necessary competence to perform any task within an organization as the elements around which to build learning and development. Because humans are social creatures, most organizations are fundamentally process driven. Those processes for a typical business would be things such as the Order-to-Cash cycle (OTC), Procure-to-Pay (P2P), Prospect to Order, and so on. These processes then form the foundation upon which the entity delivers its product or service to customers and derives value for its stakeholders. They are the basis for value creation in the economy. Why would an enterprise wish to use anything else to drive its employee-assessment and -development efforts?

Business Processes

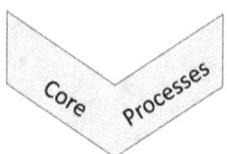

The Prospect to Order (PTO)
The Order-to-Cash (O2C) cycle
The Supply Chain Management (SCM)
The Procure to Pay (P2P)

The Pricing
The Product Management
The Accounting Cycle
Strategy/Budgeting

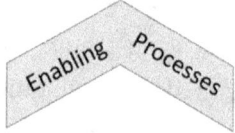

FIGURE 9: Core and Enabling Business Processes

Processes can be easily broken down into a sequential series of objective results that drive the process to a successful conclusion. These Result Areas of a process are relatively few for any given process, and they are supported by specific competencies needed within each Result Area to accomplish the objectives. These competencies may be further broken down into sub-competencies, which are the smaller, quantifiable items of competence achievable in an 8–10-minute training or assessment event. These granular items are the building blocks upon which the model is based. The order-to-cash cycle (O2C) is a process common to most businesses. It is managed over the course of time by a number of well-known professional groups. A look at the order-to-cash cycle by one of these professional groups is shown here, broken down into Result Areas:

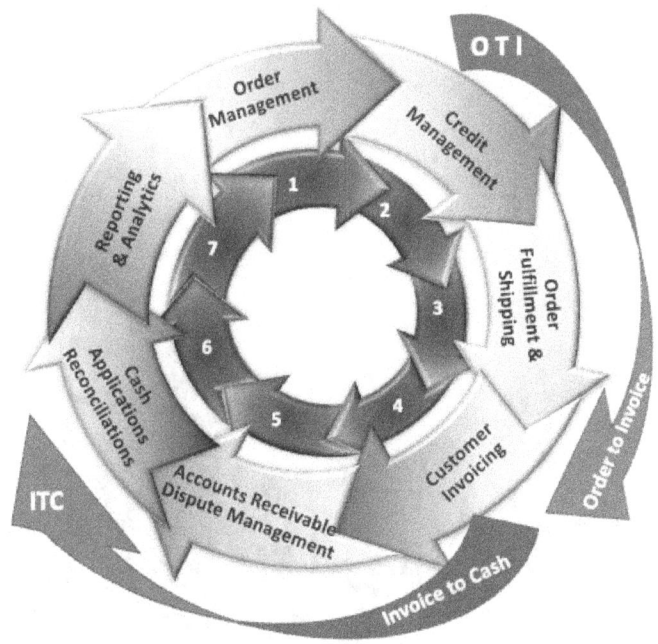

FIGURE 10: The Order to Cash Cycle (O2C)

By stacking these building blocks within a process, a business identifies the competency items that drive a given business process. By doing this for all processes within a business, a complete internal organizational competency structure is presented in support of strategy. Just as a Rubik's cube describes a three-dimensional object, these building blocks form a facet of a cube for a given process.

This facet is simply one way of looking at the blocks. If turned on its side (for instance, looking at the blocks as an educational institution), a different view of the same blocks is obtained. For instance:

Figure 11: Cube with Building Blocks (competencies) from Business Perspective

We would propose that each enterprise develop necessary strategic competencies by business function and operational competencies by process. The essence of the enterprise emerges at these intersections of function and process. Enterprises will commit to the most learning and development activities of the modern enterprise.

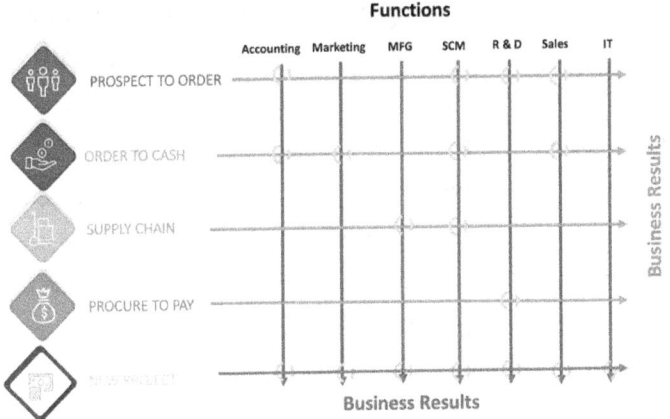

FIGURE 12: Function and Process Cross Section

Within each enterprise, other groups may take these same granular pieces and derive a different solution necessary for their environment. Just as one child's sandcastle can be made in a variety of shapes and sizes from the same grains of sand as another child's, so, too, can a government, an unemployment office, or an educational institution mold these competency blocks into a shape of their own choosing.

An educational institution must look at problems pedagogically. They, too, have a service to deliver, and that imposes certain constraints. An educational institution might look at these building blocks in an entirely different way. It may group them according to cognizant curricula and a more academic theoretical structure, but, since these building blocks are rooted in real-world needs, the institution's curriculum will be similarly rooted in and targeted toward real-world needs. Using a common framework of competencies and sub-competencies, the educational process is linked directly to economic value, a key driver of public support. As an educational institution conducts its own evolution to meet the requirements of the new millennium, it can do so knowing that these competencies are fundamental to the success of the external environment.

Figure 13: Cube with Building Blocks (competencies) from Educational Perspective

This granular model can be further enhanced by breaking down and classifying granular competencies.

BENEFITS OF ADOPTING A GRANULAR MODEL

The benefits of adopting a granular model are manifold. The primary advantage is simply that competency is immediately and currently relevant—it is what the market desires. It is the target for screening, for hiring, and for development. It is the target for educational institutions to know what is desired, and it is the target for governments to describe what they want to fund or encourage.

An employee who defines his/her skill set based upon competencies will find it easier and more productive to communicate their actual value to a potential employer. GIG-work selection of these same people is facilitated by using these same competencies. Resumes will give way to simplified marketing devices designed to gauge interest and organizational fit.

By focusing granularly, we produce a common language across organizations and across societal elements. Educational institutions, governments, businesses, and individuals may all speak about the same thing in analogous ways. The conversations developed will be more substantive and useful than the typical conversations we are having now.

The structure is scalable. If we build in this manner, it is more easily integrated with existing and developing training resources, with the GIG marketplace, and with emerging technologies like AI. Any future process and any future function can be analyzed and broken down in this manner. We can positively respond to change and avoid change representing more stress on an unworkable system.

Strategically, a business benefits from organizing via such a model. A CEO can obtain a strategic map of competency levels inside the organization, can test various strategic alternatives with their competency needs against the current reality, and model the difficulty in executing any given strategy. Most organizational-change efforts fail culturally, and a CEO would be able to assess these elements with a clearer eye.

Tactically, a business benefits by being able to granularize its internal needs into competency blocks and by offering its own internal competencies to internal needs via its own internal GIG-marketplace. An employee with an accounting background who writes well could be tasked to produce a market messaging piece, for instance. Such an internal marketplace could be easily linked to an external one, allowing that business to develop its own pool of screened, qualified, and rated ad-hoc GIG workers. This seamless integration of the greater GIG-marketplace with the internal needs of the business allows for a more responsive and lower-cost delivery of valuable outcomes.

The implications of a competency-based focus for the hiring process are profound. Resumes, which have always been primarily marketing documents, become targeted marketing instruments, and initial screening and selection components will be greatly simplified and driven by commonly agreed-upon competency assessments. Organizational fit will be the primary item to be assessed, as underlying competency will be known. The process will be a functioning one, with fewer errors and heartache for all concerned.

Governmental services benefit, as assessing and assisting the unemployed is easier. The unemployed could be facilitated through competency retraining for specific in-demand competencies. Furthermore, the unemployed can be offered a government-run GIG-marketplace, with their skills available on an ad-hoc basis to the government as well as to external parties. Governments could subsidize work through these marketplaces by keeping the unemployed engaged in the job market and rewarding work, rather than simply subsidizing unemployment, as does the current model. Governments would be able to encourage desirable behaviors on the part of employers and the unemployed.

SUMMARY AND CONCLUSIONS

- Business is based on processes. Functions serve to facilitate higher-order strategic competencies and not necessarily economic flows. Efficient processes are the basis of enterprise value creation.

- Learning-and-development platforms are currently most often based upon functions that don't match processes. This leaves these platforms with extended training and assessment processes misaligned with the daily needs of the average employee.
- Most learning-and-development training is of a longer duration and not immediately applicable to daily business. This delays satisfaction of the needs of both employees and businesses and fails to meet the needs of a dynamic marketplace.
- *Real learning takes place at the intersection of process and function*—that is, at the intersection of basic process competence and higher-order thinking and learning.
- Employees want shorter, rapidly applicable learnings which allow them to "dabble" in a number of things before deciding upon a learning direction which might then be informed by study at an educational institution.
- Educational institutions are organized by function for narrow, more technical fields like engineering, accounting, or business, e.g., the MBA, and by more generalized training such as in liberal arts, etc. These may be linked to business by integrating competency elements into their curricula.
- Societal forces are driving toward more time-limited ad-hoc arrangements (GIG work) that balances

the short-term and narrow demands of suppliers. Managers are positioned to manage outcomes on a narrower and more focused basis. A work structure that brings that clarity to this action point is useful.

- As in the case of HAL, heuristics and other forms of Artificial Intelligence are being used to automate both tasks and analysis. Removing some human intervention from certain tasks enables a higher potential for learning success and possible redirection of resources toward other processes that are less successful in an AI mode. Short, granular assessing, training, and testing processes are increasingly possible and successful, and are being deployed in the real world.

Chapter VI

A CONTEXT FOR OPTIMIZING A SCALABLE HUMAN RESOURCE POOL

The first five chapters of this book explain the general concepts and flow of construct of the pool of competencies, sub-competencies, dimensions, and levels that enable an enterprise to discover the wealth of talent in its human resource pool and to discover what talent is absent but mandatory in order for the enterprise to achieve its objectives. This is always an area of interest to stakeholders around the world.

This chapter introduces the methodology required to implement a competency-based solution to human resource challenges and a paradigm that provides a pathway to optimized human capital resources. The first relates the paradigm to education.

I. EDUCATION AND QUALIFICATION

Mutually Beneficial and Complementary Knowledge

In recent decades, researchers have focused much attention on the role and relative value of both practical and academic knowledge in creating higher-level competencies in the individual. Studies have suggested what elements of human capital enable contribution to the economy and to society[12].

It is beyond the scope of this book to delve too deeply into global educational-system constructs, but it is appropriate to consider the examples of certain countries in both Europe and America. Typically, European school curricula and proposed outcomes are controlled in partnership between the legislatures of the member states and the European Union. Each nation relates its process outcome as open to adjustment in order to secure the best value for its citizens and the national economy. Beginning with preschool training, the curricula promote a diverse and multicultural agenda, while providing a strong foundation and satisfying the needs of individuals to choose optional tracks in careers[13].

Generally, the European school system provides two years of early education (kindergarten), five years of basic education, and seven years of voluntary training. Early learners are accepted into kindergarten in September, at the start of the school year of the calendar year in which the child attains the age of four. Students progress to basic education at the age of six, beginning at the start of the school year in September of the calendar year[14].

---

12 Benhabib and Spiegel 1994; Romer 1990; Barro 2001; Hanushek and Woessmann 2008, 2010, and 2012
13 Organization of studies, 2020
14 Ibid.

Switzerland provides a national framework for the integration of practical knowledge and academic education. Through its Vocational Education and Training (VET) program, students are prepared for direct introduction into the marketplace across many critical occupations, including information technology, advanced manufacturing, and the healthcare industry, as well as traditional trades and crafts. Importantly, businesses enjoy the benefits of the training of a highly skilled workforce and the seamless connections between VET and the broader Swiss education system.

A genuine indicator of the value of the system is the fact that some 70% of the country's youth participate in the Swiss VET system. It has become a critical driver of the country's economic engine. The system attracts a broad cross-section of students—many high achievers—and facilitates the seamless integration of these successful young people into both white-collar and blue-collar careers by way of a robust apprenticeship structure. This has resulted in a low youth-unemployment rate, a rare accomplishment in these times.

While other European countries such as Germany, Austria, Denmark, and Norway have similar programs with varying levels of success, it seems that the Swiss VET program is rapidly becoming a European and possibly OECD standard.

Guided by continuing advances in education across the globe and faced with a critical need to continue learning transformation and accelerate a vision for the future, most countries have recognized the need to reform their education systems. This is a good start but hardly a final solution. The challenge now is actual implementation. The paradigm being presented in this book provides a pathway to this transformation.

Life's experiences provide a mantra that guided me throughout my career and has proven beneficial: "Knowledge has the most value when it meets individual needs within the current context of one's life."

Typical human resource organizations are tasked with evaluating and selecting critical resources for enterprises but are often overwhelmed; that pressure causes fear and delay in a very necessary process. As a consequence, talent in the form of diverse competencies will go unrecognized and untapped in favor of a narrow selection process to fill the immediate need of a very narrow functional requirement, such as "business analyst" or "reconciliation specialist." It is often the case that individual talents are multifaceted, with expertise across many different knowledge areas and at many different levels and dimensions of competency ... simultaneously. It only makes sense to secure services from individuals with the most robust inventory of knowledge, so to speak, the best price-performance.

It has become clear in our research that capability and success are not necessarily correlated to a university degree. The reality is that knowledge consists of many dimensions and that success depends most upon the ability to direct competencies to best effect in an environment that recognizes and enables this process to occur. Consider the case of the Instagram influencer. Is it necessary for an individual to hold advanced university degrees to become a world-class influencer? Often not, as it happens. When experience is overlaid upon a solid base of preparation, the influencer may share value among followers that provides an advantage in the form of preferred action to achieve the desired outcome or to avoid risk and exposure by reason of experience. Either way, an advanced degree may have little or no advantage in this instance. It may add significant value in other cases, but, in this case, the more tactile experience prevailed; thus, the reason for determining actual and desirable competencies in the formulation of a particular solution—the who, what, when, and where of resource availability.

ENTER THE DIGITAL NOMAD

The change in thinking regarding Talent Management has given rise to a number of significant market opportunities. Enter the digital nomad (DN), an individual with specific expertise available to markets in order to reduce the cost of changing focus in human resource utilization. By personal choice and supported by the restrictions of a global pandemic, these GIG laborers are growing in popularity. Platforms differ in how they promote services, but the process effectively brings together a large number of Digital Nomads capable of responding to the needs of willing buyers of their services.

Globally, the GIG economy has gained incredible momentum in the last few years. Freelancers and temporary workers are now taking advantage of the top GIG-economy companies out there, balancing flexibility with competitive wages. In 2019, staffing-industry analysts reported that world spending on GIG jobs reached a massive $4.5 trillion!

Of particular interest to Digital Nomads is the ability to position themselves in very advantageous locations, with fewer tax consequences and perhaps even less oversight. Given the market condition, this is a value that should be taken advantage of now, since government taxing authorities have an interest in mitigating the isolation Digital Nomads enjoy and securing revenue from their efforts in country. Similarly, enterprise risk arises from the lack of liability insurance of most Digital Nomads, given the nature of their model. Potential client companies subject to regulation and local taxing authorities will weigh the risk and return of selecting a Digital Nomad, as it will impose an unnecessary risk on the firm. Additionally, in today's world of system penetration and chaos, introducing an exterior risk into the company systems will almost certainly give rise to concern from the risk-management side of the business.

Some platforms, for example, Fiverr and Appen, monitor and measure productivity and customer satisfaction of each servicing e-provider and provide a modicum of protection to buyers utilizing services on their platforms. An individual provider, perhaps a Digital Nomad, receives a list of requirements and negotiates a fee with the buyer of services. Frequent communication determines that the provider understands the objective outcome, and final payment is contingent upon a satisfactory acceptance by the buyer.

DIGITAL NOMADS—THE ULTIMATE GIG SATISFIERS— ALREADY LEADING THE WAY

Digital Nomads are individuals who use available modern technologies to earn a living and who generally lead their lives as nomads, without a permanent residence. They often work from abroad, from cafés, public libraries, common rooms, or even recreational vehicles. Often this is achieved through the use of devices with wireless internet capabilities such as Smartphones or mobile hotspots. Successful Digital Nomads usually present a high degree of independence and self-discipline and manage strong work-life balance.

The Digital Nomads community consists of a wide variety of host members. During the 1970s, a common classification of the Digital Nomads included retired or semi-retired persons and seasonal transients referred to as "snowbirds." These tended to be individuals and families from the far north intent on avoiding the snow and adverse conditions of northern winters and returning to the northern fold in more advantageous months.

Individuals typically chose to become Digital Nomads to promote financial independence or to enter a career that allows for location independence. Although they enjoy advantages in terms of freedom and flexibility, a small number report loneliness as one of their greatest challenges, followed by overwork leading to eventual burnout.

Eventually, reality confronts the Digital Nomads. Mundane challenges such as securing and maintaining international health insurance with global coverage, complying with various local laws, and obtaining work visas move to the forefront. As well, the global pandemic has caused most countries to ban cross-border and international travel, leaving Digital Nomads stranded in diverse parts of the world. Despite the benefits, there are risks confronting enterprising Digital Nomads.

GENERATION NOW AND ATTITUDES TOWARD EDUCATION AND QUALIFICATION

In a conversation with a young woman on the subject of competency, work ethics, and common attitudes among employees, it became clear that she would never hire an individual without a degree or, more precisely, without presumed qualification. After the passing of the initial shock, I asked myself whether society had failed to convey proper norms and values to our young people such that would allow this person to respond in this way. By what standard is it determined that a person without a degree will not master a job for which they have been hired? It is a given that today individuals and employers feel the need to hire individuals with a degree. The premise of this book challenges that approach, instead favoring an assessment of knowledge in all of its forms, measured within a common framework, enabling agile access to the necessary mix of competencies for particular challenges.

As with all good ideas, there was a time when they represented the best option. Inquire of Adam whether the short-term satisfaction of the apple on hunger was consistent with later needs.

The original idea for the school-education process was good and innovative in its day. Over time, we have all come to agree that mostly everyone needs some kind of knowledge and of education. The original intention of schooling was to stimulate literacy and expand the general level of knowledge. As a consequence, the process was intended to stimulate increasingly higher levels of inquiry and more research and development, resulting in benefit to the general welfare of society. As humans evolved and technological advances accelerated, knowledge grew more diverse, requiring more institutions to assure availability and continuity of conduits, such as primary and secondary schools, trade schools, and universities all focused on introducing a more complete individual knowledge platform. Knowledge has long been a logical predictor of achievement and a key differentiator of satisfactory and poor outcomes.

A critical component of apparent and actual knowledge measurement is the vehicle by which such knowledge is measured. Historically, scholars introduced tests and exams through which proficiency was determined by answers provided to specific questions.

The accessibility of global, state-sanctioned tests takes into consideration the benchmarking of instructive frameworks across nations, with the point of understanding the determinants of understudy accomplishment that appears to be more identified with test scores.

There is proof that, inside a similar academic framework, a few schools acquire preferred instructive outcomes over others and that grades are reliant on different understudies' own qualities and foundation more than on tutoring.

With this attitude, have we started a discriminatory process by applying labels and marks to individuals? Attitudes such as "I have had a better upbringing and am therefore better" produced big gaps among social classes. Phrases like "Only those who have had education are cultured and socially acceptable" were frequently used globally. Lastly, we have been brought up with the statement "Only through proper schooling can you become wise and successful!"

But only the rich or the otherwise fortunate could afford school education. Organizations like the International Labor Organization[15] (ILO) have been established to survey,

---

15 https://www.ilo.org/global/about-the-ilo/history/lang--en/index.htm

guide, and structure the overall effort. In August 2010, the International Labor Organization (ILO) published its report on global employment trends for youth 2010. The report concluded that there are approximately 620 million economically active young people worldwide. At the end of 2009, 81 million of them were unemployed—eight million more than in 2007. Global levels of unemployment among young people aged from 15 to 24 are the highest on record. Now, in 2020, following ILO's recent report, young people face an uncertain future in the labor market because of automation, the narrow focus of much vocational training, and the lack of jobs to match their qualifications, says a new ILO report. The number of young people currently "Not in Employment, Education, or Training" (NEET) is rising, and young women are more than twice as likely as their male counterparts to be affected. There are currently around 1.3 billion young people globally, of whom 267 million are classified as NEET. Two-thirds, or 181 million, of NEETs are young women.

For years, education submerged into politics and become a money-generating machine, turning into a very profitable business. Nowadays, big institutions like Harvard, Oxford, Cambridge, and MIT are expanding their business to online platforms, offering studies and courses with a guaranteed certificate or degree from a famous/prominent university, reducing tuition costs and enticing young and old to pep up their CVs.

Throughout history we have alternated between changing the structure and living within it. A hierarchy of disciplines in schools is based partly on assumptions about supply and demand in the marketplace. We are at the point where the structures that have brought us this far no longer suit the needs of the 21st century.

A new economy demands a deeper conception of talent, and the organic nature of our lives demands it, too. With the arrival of ubiquitous information and rapid search, education is no longer a destination but a continuous journey. Leading educational institutions are no longer the destination for acquiring knowledge but the environment to help us synthesize the explosion of information coming our way. The two great driving forces are technological innovation and population growth. Together they are transforming how we live and work. They are putting a vast strain on the Earth's natural resources and changing the nature of politics and culture. Human affairs have always been turbulent, but what is distinctive now is the rate and scale of change. These technological changes—combined with population and climate changes—are affecting everyone on Earth, and the outcomes are essentially unpredictable. What is certain is that, in the next 50 to 100 years, children will need to confront challenges that are unique in human history.

Has the world indoctrinated us and generations to come with outmoded models and structures? The world has found ways to categorize the human race. From the moment we are born, we get titles. From a *newborn* into an *infant* into a *toddler* into *early and middle childhood* into *adolescence* and eventually into *early, middle, and late adulthood*, we are given titles. We are surrounded by categorizations and structures and standardizations. What are the underlying criteria that justify these categories? Age? Physical, emotional, spiritual, or psychological age? Size? The size of our body? The fact is that, no matter how much we brainstorm on these fixed definitions, as long as we live, we will remain part of a specific category. This is a fact we will not change easily.

From this perspective, humanity needs structural lines. That way, we can live together and alongside each other in the hope that we adapt to the structure or alter it to fit the new world. In both cases, it remains a structure. Humanity has always struggled with the need for structure and the confinement that structure itself brings. Neither we nor our parents could predict the path when we started college studies that has brought us to where we are today. The principle is the same for everyone. Life is not linear. Education is not a linear process of preparation for the future. It is about cultivating the talents and sensibilities through which we can live our best lives in the present and create the best futures for us all.

Applying this structure to parenthood and education, parents are excited and proud when their child starts school.

It is a new step in the child's world and, to be honest, a huge step for the parents' independence for at least a few hours per day. Following this pattern, society has taught us the following structure for the cycle of life: "From a newborn into an infant into a toddler into early and middle childhood, into adolescence" we are in the *dependency* phase. Our parents and the community take full responsibility for us. We are placed in schools and pushed to abide by the existing structures. During the second life cycle, "early, middle, and late adulthood," we slide into the *independent* phase. We can select the structure or categorization for our life based on what we have been shown and taught; we are responsible for our being and eventually our own offspring. The cycle closes for us and is repeated by our offspring.

Once we finish elementary school, we seek admission to a secondary educational school. Do we know what we really want to become in life? Of course, not every one of us has the chance or the drive to finish elementary school or secondary education. Internal and external factors are constantly influencing our path and decision-making. You move with your high-school degree in your hand to a higher-education institution or vocational college.

There is also the option of not finishing school. The reasons really don't matter. Let's say you finished school—you use this degree to gain admission to a higher-education institution or vocational profession training school. Along the way, you realize that this study or vocational training shows you only a small side of what you really are and want and is limiting you in your being and imagination.

With the pressure from parents and the social environment, you push through, but you acknowledge how it shortens your wings. It has already taken hold of you and begins to encase you, like spilled oil that negates a bird's ability to fly. But you persist—the degree awaits you at the end of the tunnel.

It can also go the other way: This study or vocational training shows you your full potential, and it satisfies your inspiration and enthusiasm completely. You become one with your study or profession, and it turns into a vocation. In the word "vocational" hides the word "vocation," which means "a calling" or something that draws you forward, connoting the dedication or passion that leads to emotional fulfillment.

No matter how your higher education or vocational training ends, you now reach the age and maturity to stand on your own feet and earn your own money. Some of you may have done this already. Now it's time for another exchange—your higher degree or vocational certificate can be exchanged for employment—a job. But we are not one dimensional. Are we humans defined only by the evidence of our achievements, such as a degree? Ken Robinson said that, in 1950, students with good high-school qualifications expected a life of stable employment, perhaps staying with the same company until retirement.

But that is unlikely now. In some ways, you are still better off with a degree than without one, but it will only get you started in the job market. It doesn't give you security once you are there. Graduates who find work in 2018 will not expect to be with the same company in 2050 or even that the company will still be around then.

The instructive structure from elementary, auxiliary, postsecondary training, including college, proficiency training, professional training, specialized school, to postdoctoral investigation and exploration basically stayed the same, aside from little changes and alterations. Surveying the business condition, we see that learning-and-development experts are looking for direction to adjust to the new age and business requirements. Entrenched attitudes, institutions, and structures are hard to change.

Can a degree or certificate give one enough vocational-education preparation to follow the work path? With the appearance of the European Union, nations have put forth an astounding attempt at adjusting instructive strategies, ways, and degrees. Several organizations have aimed to find the "golden path" that raises commitment and perseverance in individuals' education and profession. One of these organizations is "CEDEFOP,"[16] established in 1975 by Council Regulation (EEC). The organization's objective is the development of vocational and educational

---

16 https://www.cedefop.europa.eu/en

training (VET). Its endeavors are centered around expertise advancement and exploration, and supporting collaboration and shared learning among European and public VET policymakers, social accomplices, analysts, suppliers, and specialists. CEDEFOP considers vocational education and training the key to integrating individuals effectively into the universe of work, demonstrating that individuals need the correct capabilities to secure positions.

Individuals with low degrees of or no capability are almost multiple times bound to be jobless than those with high capabilities. In their ongoing report from 2019, CEDEFOP showed that, in the EU, around 75 million individuals, almost 33% of the working population, have low or no capability.

Further, CEDEFOP asserted that a large number of youngsters, around 15%, leave school with no capabilities—more precisely, with no *degree*. Yet, organizations request individuals with the abilities needed to compete and consistently work at a high level.

A few nations within the EU have high unemployment rates among qualified youngsters, and other countries have a high demand for qualified youngsters. From my own experience, as an educator at a vocational college, guiding students through apprenticeships, I recognized the differentiations between vocational training (the so-called professional preparing) and genuine, real-world business life. With this in mind, it is justified to ask how well VET bridges the gap between educational/vocational training and the genuine business world. We must re-examine the role of these organizations in our societies and the desired outcomes for the new millennium.

The educational system, as it has been established, with grades, labels, and ideas was predominant in preparing future workers/employees for the job market. Similarly, evaluations, grades, and labels encouraged a mindset of position, title, and compensation.

Following Samuel Johnson's definition of a "job," we all want to contribute to society and are prepared to measure our three-to-four-year study or vocational training against Johnson's definition of "a low affair." Genuinely enough, we need and want to earn our own living, substantiate ourselves as strong citizens and members of society, and add to its prosperity.

The school system has not yet been adequately adapted to contemporary, new challenges and generational changes for the centuries to come. Somewhere along the way, we have lost sight of the obvious: Knowledge is useful only if it is applied to a purpose. Knowledge applied to a purpose is at the root of competence. We are remiss today for not recognizing that our fundamental societal objective is to cultivate the competencies necessary for our societies to survive and thrive in the fast-paced environment of this new millennium.

In my experience, "education" in the hiring process is often simply a proxy to fill in for the ineffectiveness of the process itself. It becomes a crutch. Our difficulty in identifying precisely the competencies that we must have is a result of simply being in a rush. We ask for a particular degree so that we do not have to think. No HR leader has been criticized for bringing a candidate with a degree forward. The process leaves some highly competent candidates on the sidelines. Organizations of tomorrow will need to be "Twitch-Agile" and ready to reconfigure themselves and respond rapidly to unexpected challenges. Whether considering internal full-time employees, short-term contractors, or outsourced suppliers, organizations need to develop for themselves a "GIG Marketplace," where competencies are well known and assessed. These marketplaces will allow rapid change, effective hiring or sourcing, and reconfiguration to any strategy an organization may adopt.

The process began with the development of a common vocabulary and process through which to assess and determine proficiency, or, more commonly, verifiable competency. Sir Ken Robinson has formulated it this way: "When you follow your own true north, you create new opportunities, meet different people, have different experiences, and create a different life."

II. BUSINESS PROCESS AND COMPETENCY

A review of the Business Process Cycle as shown below under Figure 14 and the diagram including the Order-to-Cash Cycle as shown under Figure 15 provide a refreshing understanding of the puzzle that is enterprise business process. In order to establish competency, each general area, herein referred to as Result Areas, requires certain talent, experience, skills, and education in order to maximize the value of each and every human resource.

In time, a complete common vocabulary and framework will be refined to enable an enterprise of any size to select the key features of human support that it currently requires or, as a result of succession planning, will require at key points in time. Establishing a vehicle and process to provide a solution to this dilemma has begun with this book.

The previous section addressed the challenge in education. Here, in this section, we deconstruct the major Result Areas of common Business Processes as encountered in enterprises/organizations and provide granularity to the theories previously shared.

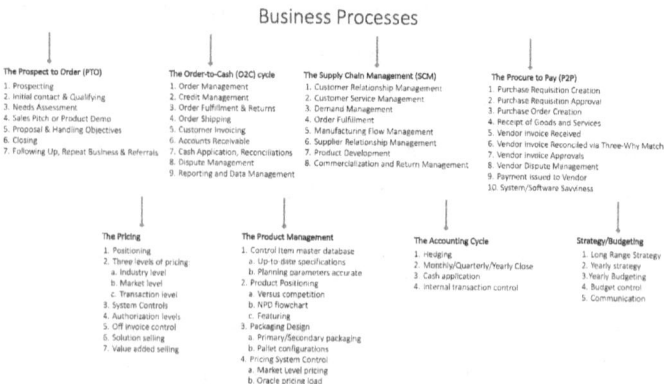

Figure 14: Core and Enabling Business Processes

A CONTEXT FOR OPTIMIZING... | 163

A COMPETENCY MODEL FOR THE BUSINESS PROCESS ORDER-TO-CASH (O2C CYCLE)

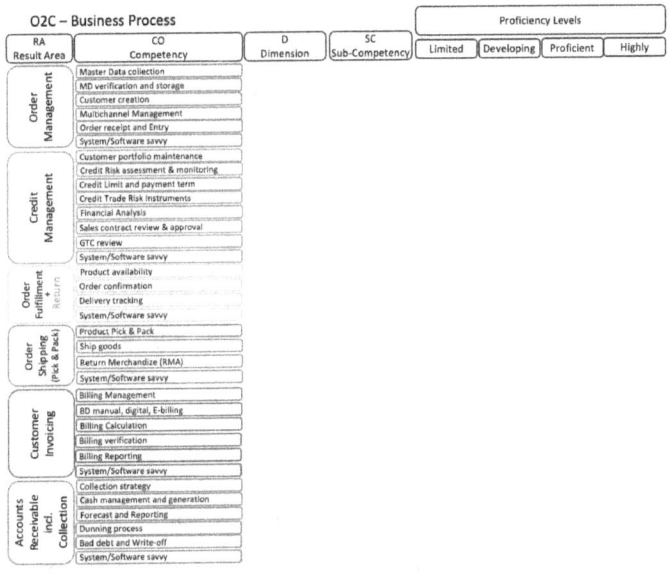

FIGURE 15: O2C Competency Model

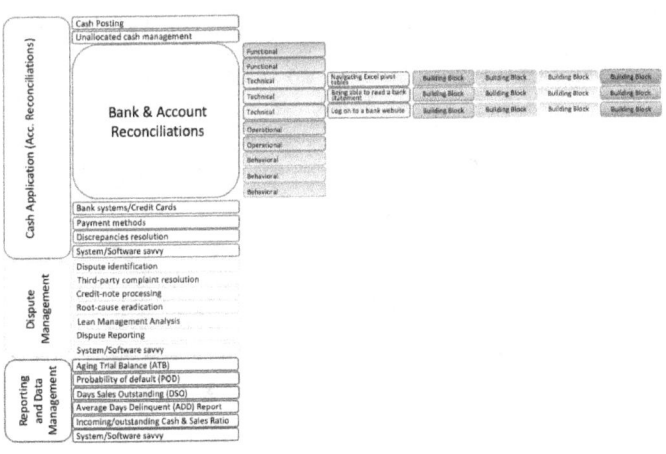

FIGURE 16: O2C Competency Model

As a start, on the following pages we will present the eight most common Business Processes segmented in their Result Areas.

PROSPECT TO ORDER (PTO)

Also referred to as the "Sales process" or "Quote-to-Order" (Q2O) and generally as "the revenue generator." From the myriad of PTO overviews found online, we decided to display one of the most detailed and precise overviews on PTOs formulated by Act!365[17]. Sales are the lifeblood of every organization, and a sales process streamlines the activities and allows clear visibility and transparency. A sales process is a repeatable sequence of stages, each including a set of actions that sales representatives perform to convert a potential customer from a lead to a paying customer. It acts as a road map to keep your team members on track, so they always know what to do next, without hesitation. Here we will review a seven-step sales process.

1. Prospecting: Leads are found through prospecting, also known as lead generation
2. Initial Contact and Qualifying: Via a phone call, email, or social media
3. Needs Assessment: A series of standard open-ended questions prepared to ask prospects

---

17 https://www.act365.com/7-step-sales-process/

4. Sales Pitch or Product Demo: Communicate the value of the solution in terms of the prospect's needs
5. Proposal and Handling Objectives: Customized to prospect's needs, challenges, motivations
6. Closing: Prospects commit to purchase or stop the process; is not a stand-alone event
7. Following Up, Repeat Business, and Referrals: Nurture an ongoing relationship

Process explanation includes:

1. Prospect through marketing methods, networking at live events or trade shows as well as on social media, purchased lists, cold calling, and referrals to identify potential buyers.
2. Gather key information to determine if leads are a good match for the product or service. Qualifying questions are typically related to budget, authority, need, and timeline
3. The goal is to thoroughly understand the prospect's situation, challenges, and motivations; allows upfront tailoring of the sales pitch or demo to each specific prospect
4. Connecting the potential customer's needs with the corresponding features and benefits of the product offering
5. Focus on the aspects that are of greatest value to the potential customer, and highlight how it will

help to reach their desired outcome. Keep a record of objections and prepare possible answers

6. Sale is made; prospects either agree on your terms and price or negotiate for mutually beneficial ones. All details are finalized for delivery, fulfillment, or related actions, and introduced to those who will be handling the next steps
7. Continue relationship through marketing communications such as updates about new offerings, industry news, an e-newsletter, or some sort of interactive rewards program. Terrific source of referrals

ORDER-TO-CASH (O2C) CYCLE

The O2C cycle, also referred to as OTC, belongs to the heartbeat processes and is the most critical and complex one of any organization; it is the most outsourced business process. The reference "OTC" can be misleading, due to the same abbreviation used in the pharmaceutical industry for medical drugs that are sold "over the counter." The term is OTC—Over the Counter.

The O2C cycle covers the whole process, from order entry to cash allocation, and is mostly known as the sum of "OTI"—Order to Invoice—and "ITC"—Invoice to Cash. Its industry group has defined eight Result Areas as O2C's logical components, whereas some organizations create an additional area. Among the process descriptions found online, we aligned the most with the description from BCG[18]. These are:

1. Order Management
2. Credit Management
3. Order Fulfillment and Returns
4. Order Shipping
5. Customer Invoicing
6. Accounts Receivable
7. Cash Application—Cash Posting, Reconciliations
8. Dispute Management
9. Reporting and Data Management

Process explanation includes:

1. Master Data collection, verification, and storage; customer creation; multichannel management; receiving and entering orders from customer via email, Internet, salesperson, fax, or by some form of electronic data interchange
2. Customer portfolio, credit risk assessment and monitoring, credit limit and payment term, credit trade risk instruments, financial analysis, sales contract review (long-term or short-term), GTC review

---

18 https://www.bcg.com/en-ch/publications/2020/order-to-cash-platforms-are-the-future

3. Product availability, order confirmation, and delivery tracking
4. Product Pick & Pack, shipping goods, return merchandise authorization (RMA) management
5. Billing management, manual, digital, e-billing, calculation, verification, reporting
6. Collection strategy, cash management and generation, forecasting and reporting, dunning process, bad debt and write-off
7. Cash posting, reconciliations, unallocated cash management, discrepancies resolution, bank systems/credit cards, payment methods
8. Dispute identification, third party-complaint resolution, credit-notes processing, root-cause eradication, lean management analysis
9. Aging trial balance (ATB) and probability of default (POD), days sales outstanding (DSO) and average days delinquent (ADD) report, incoming/outstanding cash and sales ratio

SUPPLY CHAIN MANAGEMENT (SCM)

Supply Chain Management (SCM) is defined as the design, planning, execution, control, and monitoring of supply-chain activities with the objective of creating net value, building a competitive infrastructure, leveraging worldwide logistics, synchronizing supply with demand, and measuring performance globally. SCM draws heavily from the areas of operations management, logistics, procurement, and information technology, and strives for an integrated approach.

1. Customer Relationship Management
2. Customer Service Management
3. Demand Management
4. Order Fulfillment
5. Manufacturing Flow Management
6. Supplier Relationship Management
7. Product Development
8. Commercialization and Return Management

PROCURE TO PAY (P2P)

Generally, enterprises require either raw materials or services sourced from outside the enterprise in order to initiate the process of order fulfillment. The P2P process executes the steps necessary to acquire the requisite quality and amount from credible sources in an efficient manner. Once received and integrated into the inventory, this cycle further assures a payment within terms in order to secure the timely access of future sourced materials or services.

The Result Areas of this cycle include:

1. Purchase Requisition Creation
2. Purchase Requisition Approval
3. Purchase Order Creation

4. Receipt of Goods and Services
5. Vendor Invoice Received
6. Vendor Invoice Reconciled via Three-Wy Match
7. Vendor Invoice Approvals
8. Vendor Dispute Management
9. Payment Issued to Vendor
10. System/Software Savviness

PRICING

A critical component of the business cycle involves the determination of the actual cost to produce the value, goods, or services, in order to establish a profit margin for the sales process. It is important that the selected margin represent cover for production and service cost plus an element of profit. Proper pricing controls keep an enterprise from predation, that is, selling into the market at a price at or below enterprise cost to produce. The process has analytical, experiential, and control requirements, but competency in each is an absolute requirement for a going concern. The Result Areas involved include:

1. Positioning
2. Three levels of pricing:
    a. Industry level
    b. Market level
    c. Transaction level
3. System Controls

4. Authorization levels
5. Off invoice control
6. Solution selling
7. Value-added selling

PRODUCT MANAGEMENT

Vital to enterprise success is the substance, presentation, and delivery of the best product to the right markets. Often referred to as Product Marketing, this cycle of interaction assures that each product is properly classified, described, and inventoried at the best possible physical location in order to best respond to orders, regardless of volume. As market analysis is constantly executed and reviewed, adjustment to key features assures that pricing, manufacturing point to physical-inventory location, and strategy continue relevant as implemented in the fiscal period.

The key Result Areas include:

1. Control Item master database
    a. Up-to-date specifications
    b. Planning parameters accurate
2. Product Positioning
    a. Versus competition
    b. NPD flowchart
    c. Featuring
3. Packaging Design
    a. Primary/Secondary packaging

    b. Pallet configurations
4. Pricing System Control
    a. Market Level pricing
    b. Oracle pricing load

FINANCE AND ACCOUNTING

The lifeblood of any enterprise is its capital, be it cash flow or debt sourcing, each critical to assuring that an enterprise maintains operations and payroll, and satisfies its creditors as debt falls due. Beyond the traditional cash-flow imperative is the requirement to secure the best cost of debt from each of the myriad vehicles: short-, medium-, and long-term funding sources that supplement the conversion of invoicing to cash. Traditionally a Finance function, they enable the group to manage global hedging programs to assure capital availability throughout the enterprise. In addition, the accounting group assures proper consolidation, classification, and reporting of all assets according to GAAP standards, and protects the reputational capital of the enterprise. Relevant Result Areas include:

1. Cash management, including cash application
2. Monthly/Quarterly/Yearly Close
3. Hedging
4. Internal transaction control
5. Ledger management

STRATEGY/BUDGETING

In order to maintain proper achievement in an organization, it is necessary to analyze and report current condition, as measured against past strategy, and adjust accordingly in order to achieve enterprise objectives. This requires the establishment of a budget along with each plan to assure a measurement process that identifies deviation and the need for correction. The fiscal reporting mechanism established for each major enterprise assures that there is both internal and external stakeholder visibility and communication of the rationale, decisions taken, and outcome achieved by leadership. The key result areas include:

1. Long-Range Strategy
2. Yearly Strategy
3. Yearly Budgeting
4. Budget Control
5. Communication

Epilogue

The Journey Continues

The paradigm becomes the next step in Human Resource Capital (HRC) optimization.

- Talent availability
- Cost efficiency
- Competitive advantage
- Risk management across markets
- The end game of continuous improvement

When we set out to discuss this topic, we reflected upon our experience consulting in the field, assisting with process improvement and training in businesses and shared service centers. We had encountered numerous companies with challenges in their learning-and-development systems and structures. There is a lot of pressure on those organizations to reduce costs, provide better content, link to real-world needs, and reduce risk. From our perspective, the biggest risk faced by learning-and-development organizations is the obsolescence risk of their own work product. Many providers barely get the delivery of one structure and its associated deliverables completed before a strategic organizational change demands a change in the response from the learning-and-development teams. It didn't seem logical that such wholesale change was required. This caused us to reflect upon the basis for the structures adopted in the first place and to understand what precisely these teams in the field were actually doing. What was really valuable, and what were the enduring elements? What were the needs of the team members and the enterprise? Our conclusions have been developed at length in this book.

During an engagement with an international organization, we were tasked with identifying the cause for high costs in deploying workers internationally. The root cause was found to be inconsistent definitions among the various groups of what specific competencies were required to perform the job, what certification of those competencies were needed, and what competencies were already available in the labor pool. A simple lack of defined competencies and the inability to effectively train to required competencies caused a notable increase in expenditure, as, almost invariably, high-cost choices were made. Reflecting on this and how businesses might benefit from the experience also informed our discussions in this book.

The recommendation to replace a workplace structure that has evolved via the input of millions of people over many hundreds of years with a new basis can seem a bit arrogant. It is indeed arrogant to think that one's own judgment can supplant the judgment of so many others over so much time and distance. But the system we have is increasingly unworkable, and there is little logical basis to repair it. It is a derived and received system and not the product of design. We are faced with a situation where growth hurts, and we are not ready for the future. Moreover, the existing structure is about to undergo more stress, more rapidly than at any comparable period in history. We have provided a competency-based alternative precisely because change does not impair the model. What are the next steps then? What are the implications?

The drivers for the future are the same as they have always been:

- talent retention
- cost effectiveness
- risk reduction
- continuous improvement

These are unlikely to change and will likely only become more urgent. Furthermore, the very rationale for work and the structures of the organization are being redefined at a rapid pace. The pandemic has forced organizations to adopt distance at precisely the time in history when technology was prepared to respond. The internet boom of the late

1990s caused a massive, rapid infrastructure buildout, and the resulting bust caused a write-down of the costs of that infrastructure. Those events primed the world for rapid change in the subsequent decades and allowed the explosion of the shared-service-center model. The recovery from this pandemic will bring just such a realignment in the decades to come.

Much has changed, but we have seen only the barest hints of the possibilities so far. What were seen as barriers a little more than a year ago are now obviously not so, and we are aware of some of the trade-offs made. We know better also the usefulness of face-to-face engagement and have a better sense of its worth. We will be well positioned to transition back and forth as needed. Organizational preparation for natural disasters has been enhanced, and, much to the chagrin of children everywhere, snow days are no longer synonymous with free days.

Business offices will be forever changed as headquarters shrink or are eliminated, commute times are reduced, and work is able to be integrated into other aspects of our lives. GIG work is arriving at a rapid pace, and organizations need to think about how to respond to that. While a manufacturing process may be difficult to break down in that fashion, any other type of support or analytical work is able to be broken down into deliverable pieces and dispersed in both geography and time. The best competitors will learn how to integrate GIG work into their business model to make themselves more responsive and lower costs. The slack labor in any organization is more easily addressed.

Businesses need to view GIG work as an integral element to the rest of their future business, providing unavailable niche skills on an ad hoc basis as well as competent labor pools to meet surges in processes at lower cost. If businesses also look at their internal labor structures in a GIG-friendly manner, they will generate their own internal GIG marketplace to better utilize the competencies already extant in their workforce to a better effect. Each of us can recall meeting someone in business who had a unique skill largely unknown to their company. With an internal GIG market, businesses can better utilize the slack labor that every organization inevitably carries. Learning and Development, targeted at competencies in small, manageable pieces, would allow employees to develop new skills, to cross-train, and use these to advantage internally within the enterprise.

All employees would be developed, and that development would directly assist in creating value. Companies that prepare their internal marketplace to handle GIG will be much more adept at integrating external GIG to their business. They could utilize third-party providers like Fiverr or simply develop their own pool of self-certified GIG workers. Businesses need to be prepared for what will be a very rapid change in the labor landscape in the 21st century. The labor picture in 2050 will look almost nothing like the picture in 1950.

Governments can use a common competency model to determine what institutions, markets, and skills to encourage. Societal needs will be different as more citizens are GIG workers, with less physical attachment to the enterprise. The rise of distance work will challenge government systems of unemployment, social assistance, and even taxation. Governments can subsidize whole industries, as in the past, but they can also subsidize particular competencies of workers and change the manner in which they exert their collective will on national societies. There will be more choices.

Government services such as unemployment and social care can be reimagined in a GIG-work environment. The unemployed can be encouraged to gain new competencies and to test those competencies, and their interest in them, in the GIG marketplace. Obtaining a new job will no longer be binary, employed or unemployed, but digital, as workers can move to a new job via a series of short-term GIGs. They can enhance current competencies or develop new ones that are in demand.

Furthermore, government services can break down their own processes, as we have outlined, and establish their own GIG pools of workers to help manage surges in demand for their own services and to encourage the unemployed to work. For instance, unemployment assistance can be tied to working 5–10 hours per week in GIG assignments that could receive additional subsidy from the government but still be cheaper than hiring additional staff. The pool of GIG workers could be actively marketed to regional businesses as a way to get local talent that is "tested" before being hired permanently and as a way of integrating more flexible GIG workers than other sources (no barriers of language, time zone, custom, or preference).

Educational institutions are similarly challenged but at a far more basic level. The very rationale for an educational institution is being challenged. Educational Institutions were developed and centralized because of the huge economies obtained by concentrating the thought leaders, their intellectual work product, and the infrastructure to house them. Barriers to entry arose over time and were rather easily maintained. We attended educational institutions largely because that was where the knowledge, and those most able to assist us in assimilating it, resided. We built massive edifices to learning that essentially operated as distinct societies within society at large. We replicated existing services (gyms, medical facilities, etc.) to provide for these institutions and maintain these barriers to entry.

Many of those rationales are no longer valid or are significantly less valid than they once were. The economics of education was historically a particularly horrible one: as actual costs like salaries, etc. rose, educational costs rose faster than inflation. Fundamentally, you could not keep adding students to a classroom to defray the cost increases; it was a structurally inefficient model that in the past few decades has been rising in cost far faster than inflation. Each lesson given was largely a one-off with limited efficiency gained over time. Those cost barriers are under attack by technology, connectivity, and informational ubiquity. Educational institutions are rapidly migrating their offerings to distance learning at a fraction of the previous cost via services such as edX.

One talented educator can reach far more students, far more easily in this manner. Lessons are not a one-off, and some of the greatest minds are available to a far larger audience. The training, assessment, and testing are completed far more simply and at lower cost. The audience for an educational institution will be able to grow far larger with the same or less infrastructure. The value of in-person learning is being reassessed, and we will arrive at a balance in the coming decades that will look far different than the balance of previous decades. The educational picture in 2050 will bear only a partial resemblance to the picture of 1950.

As these institutions wrestle with their future mission and focus, they must link their outcomes more closely to real-world needs and evolve their offerings to be more smorgasbord and ad hoc. In short, they need closer integration with the real-world needs of the people and institutions that pay their bills.

Educator Ken Robinson outlined his vision for a future with limited structure to learning and the ability to explore as a central tenet. The future must match that vision because the speed of change will only increase, and the model will need to change with it. The building blocks, like grains of sand, allow any structure to be changed by people, and will look like any future vision that we choose to adopt. Ken Robinson largely rejected structure because, once put in place, it is confining.

Any future model must make changing and redefining structure simple, quick, and easy . . . agile. Just as a child may mold grains of sand into a sandcastle one day and the next day mold these same grains into an office building, so may small competency pieces be remodeled and refashioned as our thinking evolves.

Artificial Intelligence (AI) is already beginning to rework our systems and processes. A granular competency-based approach allows AI to begin to work on the learning-and-development process itself. We can rapidly develop a library of commonly accepted competencies that can be adopted by a new business much as someone buys a can of soup at the grocery store. As new processes are designed and broken down into building blocks and old ones are evolved by their respective professional societies, we can use AI to help us shift, mold, and evolve the training and assessment resources. We will spend our efforts to ensure that the new knowledge is captured in an assessable and deliverable manner. Learning-and-development organizations will not be focused on developing output for existing problems or rehashing materials to support an organizational change but will be forward focused. It will, in fact, drive and facilitate productive change.

We remain on the cusp of a period of great change with encouraging possibilities. Work structures will require adjustment to provide human resources with an ability to interface with and improve them. Prepare for an exciting journey.

As the paradigm becomes widely accepted and gives rise to a broader audience, further questions will surface, demanding additional research and adjustment to the model.

For example, will the current competency dictionary be sufficiently adaptable to accept the terminology of current practice? Does this quantum enhancement lead to optimization or merely greater complexity . . . and change, in terms of lower-level change-agent role and commitment to the outcome? Will enterprises commit the necessary resources to further align the competency paradigm to their unique requirements? Will top-level executives introduce the value into the enterprise strategic-planning process and secure maximum value from the human resource pool?

Does the period of transition to the new paradigm provide sufficient business-continuity protection, particularly in human resource utilization?

Will sufficient granularity be provided by the model to enable assessment of the value of rethinking the disposition of internal resources and, additionally, incorporating external resources more effectively to optimize the development of the enterprise?

Will the estimated economic efficiencies of talent utilization recommended by the paradigm result in return on investment sufficient to promote investment in a more extensive model?

Will the paradigm implementation be impacted by a general early lack of competency-strong human capital to complete the GIG aspect of the paradigm, in the interest of enterprises?

Will sufficient enterprise system development keep pace with the opportunity to utilize the paradigm toward the necessary agility to respond to changing market conditions?

How will the implementation of the competency paradigm enhance or even supplant current enterprise risk-management processes?

Appendix I

INSTITUTIONAL SUPPORT FOR THE UNEMPLOYED
A Continuing Missed Opportunity

CURRENTLY UNEMPLOYED... WHAT IS THE NEXT STEP?

U*nemployment is a condition* that affects not only the individual but everyone with whom they have contact, such as the community, city, or country. Both governmental (GO) and non-governmental (NGO) organizations have been established to focus on and hopefully resolve the problems of the unemployed and were founded specifically to alleviate the pressure on society posed by this challenge and its negative impact. The governmental policies of many countries attempt to deal with labor-market issues through individual systems such as the Unemployment Insurance Act or the Employment Agency Act supplemented by employment statistics.

Supported by state subsidies, organizations have tried to help the unemployed with educational, social, and financial support, assisting them in the identification of skills that enable new or different employment pathways. Since unemployment has continually represented a growing crisis around the world and, most recently, has been compounded by the pandemic, more pressure is being placed upon organizational resources to find solutions.

Existing guidelines require re-examination and adaptation in order to be suitable as solutions under current conditions, to provide current unemployed the necessary optimism and hope to present those competencies properly and positively. To assist in this process, the authors have analyzed a select number of governmental organizations that are currently encumbered by the existing unemployment problem. These include the Swiss Labor Office, the German Federal Labor Office, and the US Department of Labor.

In Switzerland, the key cog in operationalizing government unemployment and labor-market issues at the federal level is the Swiss Labor Market Authority, which is part of the Secretariat for Economic Affairs (SECO) at the Economics Ministry. It is they who determine the applicable type of systems such as the Unemployment Insurance Act and the Employment Placement Act. The Swiss unemployment cushion functions within established policies formulated by SECO and municipal governments. The Swiss government provides three essential benefits systems for persons of working age: unemployment benefits, invalidity insurance, and social assistance systems.

Unemployment and invalidity insurance are provided through contributory insurance schemes and administered by local authorities. All employees in Switzerland remit into an unemployment fund, and benefits are granted to unemployed individuals for a period of 12 months to two years, with strict compliance to government policies that vary with age, duration, and employability status. The labor offices in the cantons administer the registration process of the unemployed and provide services to jobseekers, including employment brokering, placement, counseling services, and matching candidates to reported vacancies.

Throughout the United States of America, labor and unemployment issues remain a thorny issue in every election cycle. The US Department of Labor's unemployment insurance program is a joint state-federal program that is intended to provide cash benefits to eligible workers. The maximum number of weeks payable under the program varies by state but generally consists of cover for 26 weeks. Additionally, the program operates several job-search portals, such as "CareerOne Stop" or "CareerLink" that are part of the American Job Center Network, enabling access to a database for job-related issues throughout the states, across the country. The US government has also established educational programs and vocational training centers to return unemployed individuals between 25 and 35 to the workforce, promoting new skills and opportunities for both self-employment and gainful employment as skilled labor.

In Germany, the Federal Labor Office directs Federal Government policies in the labor market established by the Hartz I–IV legislative package. The German government provides unemployment benefits (Arbeitslosengeld I) for any person who has been contributing to the German Social Security system. Unemployment benefits—"Arbeitlosengeld II"—applies to unemployed individuals who fail to qualify for Arbeitslosengeld I and are further unable to provide for their families on their current income.

In the early 2000s, the German government undertook extensive labor market reforms restructuring the Federal labor office and providing a new system of unemployment benefits, introducing personnel Services Agencies ("job search institutions") to assist in finding employment for citizens.

As a result of pilot projects introduced by the Federal Minister of Labor in 2014 and introduced nationwide in 2015, unemployment in Germany has been reduced to a pre-pandemic all-time low. To sustain important professional practices in markets, a central risk factor for long-term unemployment, employer subsidies were granted targeting unqualified individuals and intended to process individuals through a capacity-building process, including counseling. ("Grundsicherung für Arbeitslose," 2020)

A particular project overseen by the Federal Employment Agency in collaboration with the Federal Government in 2013 was aimed at young unemployed individuals 25 to 35 years old. The program was intended to provide education programs from the German dual education system and combine apprenticeships in companies with institutions' general training.

("Corona-Virus: Grundsicherung durch Arbeitslosengeld II—Bundesagentur für Arbeit," 2020)

Many federal labor offices have proposed individual and country-specific solutions to tackle unemployment. Responding to the proposals, the European Union (EU), the council of European member states, has committed considerable attention to assist vulnerable individuals in job seeking. Once unemployment is acknowledged as a serious problem affecting many if not all countries, many solutions have been proposed and have been successful, but with short-term durations.

Impacted by the pandemic, many countries now experience or continue to face a critical rise in unemployed individuals to the extent that it is impacting national GDP. The impact on individuals of being unemployed, many for the first time, is debilitating for individual self-esteem and motivation and can cause continuing misery and family disruption in the home. These problems range from aggressive behavior toward family members, even and especially children, to more public outbreaks of violence and an increased suicide rate.

During such great unemployment periods, labor officers (job center employees) offer services to assigned unemployed individuals aimed at cushioning the impact of a job loss, including counseling and assistance with job search. The work of employment officers seems under these circumstances to be not only endless but also an impossible challenge. Grants in aid from the country help to some extent, to remedy the financial disaster, but the emotional toll on individuals leaves employees discouraged and, in many cases, exhausted.

As previously explained, these employment offices and job centers supported by job officers in many countries are resourced to assist the unemployed to reintegrate into the workplace, through job placement. An employment office usually handles the registration of job seekers as well as vacancies identified from organizations in the area around the local employment office. Unemployed persons access these opportunities through a special portal established at nearly all unemployment offices.

Upon review, it would appear that, logically, every labor-market authority, intent upon the complete employment of its citizens, would endeavor to reintegrate job seekers quickly into the labor market. In doing so, the process promotes cooperation between institutions relevant to the labor market and potential hiring entities through a combination of job placement and staff leasing. The aim of these measures is to promote the quick and longer-term reintegration of the unemployed into the labor market. The result of a successful program should improve employability, strengthen the professional qualifications of the insured according to the needs of the labor market, reduce the risk of long-term unemployment, and, in the process, allow the insured to gain professional experience.

In order to meet the needs of the unemployed, labor-market solutions must be presented in different ways: courses, employment internships to gain initial work experience, temporary employment in the secondary labor market, or, in special cases, as part of a wage cost-sharing program wherein costs are shared during the first few months of work, etc.

ARE LABOR-MARKET AUTHORITIES TAKING FULL ADVANTAGE OF HIGHLY QUALIFIED AND SKILLED UNEMPLOYED INDIVIDUALS?

We have seen that many global countries have already attacked rising unemployment, and many have reduced it. The European Union and Europe in general have had successes in mitigating unemployment in its member states. Through a combination of labor-market flexibility, employment subsidies, full work weeks, improved geographical mobility and stricter performance requirements, major strides are being made in the battle for full employment.

Furthermore, educational programs and a variety of training allows unemployed individuals to acquire new skills, improving the potential for finding employment in a variety of developed and developing industries. All these measures contribute to a solution but fall short of meeting the needs of the highly skilled unemployed who, for example, have held long-term management positions or have very high qualifications, or both.

Though this may affect only a small part of the population, individuals with high capability and qualifications with long-term experience in management, generally of a more senior age, have the experience and expertise to drive productivity and the economy more effectively. Even though these are fewer across an economy, they nevertheless represent a stronger and more immediate contribution to success, generating more employment across the economy.

THE FOLLOWING EXAMPLE PRESENTS SUCH A CASE

The 58-year-old former finance director of a prosperous company—call him "David"—has been informed he will be laid off due to a restructuring of the company. Since he has been with the company for more 15 years, he receives a good severance payment. David is married, with three children attending university in different stages (years of study).

His work commitment to the company required many hours of work per week, which left little time for him to establish relationships outside the company or to enjoy a close family circle. Since his wife cared for their children and his salary provided a good quality of life, the whole family lived well on his compensation, salary, and bonus. The family resided in a modest home, a condominium consistent with his position.

David calculates that the severance payment received would cover all costs, including school expenses, for a full year. He was firmly convinced that someone with his skills and résumé, as well as his reputation, coming from such a firm, would see a quick job replacement. He adjusted his social network profile and indicated clearly that he was seeking employment.

In his well-established financial situation and as a job seeker, he had enough time to refurbish the house. Half a year had passed without any prospect of a job when friends suggested that he enroll in the local unemployment office. He turned down this opportunity, firmly believing that only the summer break had prevented him from finding a job. Calls to former co-workers and friends reinforced his conviction that he would soon find a job. He graduated with a degree in economics and spent his entire career in finance, adapting to new technologies and mastering fluency in three languages. His references and recommendations attest to his exceptional skills.

Through a friend, he finds and applies to a position equivalent to his previous one, with similar job description but lower salary. He is invited to the screening interview, where he encounters two young Human Resource employees who ask the usual interview questions. Following a forty-five-minute interview, he departs with a confirmation he will be further contacted by the company. After a three-week hiatus, he receives an email to the effect that he has not been shortlisted because he is overqualified for this position.

He will experience this situation several times over the next five months. Financially at the edge of his severance and with family savings near exhaustion, the reality has presented the need to enroll with the unemployment office. Now officially registered as unemployed, he will proceed to complete countless documents and be informed regarding the daily benefit rate to which he and his family are entitled, and the period of time to be covered. Also, he is informed of the weekly application obligation for which he is responsible to maintain his benefits. This issue is discussed at a family meeting, and it is determined that the family would have to use savings in order to cover current monthly expenses.

After nearly two years of monthly meetings with the labor-market officer and numerous applications and interviews through the unemployment office, he remained unemployed. Is this possible? Given the talent, skills, and high competencies and talent, how is it possible that he remains unemployed?

Switzerland's Unemployment Insurance Act regulates the disposition of the unemployed, including how the individual unemployment agencies are recording/registering the "skills" of the registered unemployed individuals. But does this, in fact, enable the market to identify and appreciate the knowledge and the competency of the unemployed individual? If there is a registration system, how and where have David's skills been registered? How is this accessed both by the unemployed and by prospective employers? Is the registration based only on his CV, degrees, and work certificates, and, if so, how does this translate into actionable intelligence for both potential employee and hiring enterprise?

Are registrations managed in a system only at the local level or shared with other unemployment offices? Is there a regular exchange among labor-office officials and other labor-office agencies nationwide? Is there an interaction among local hiring enterprises to identify opportunities among recruiting offices and the surrounding companies? Is there any exchange at all? Have the potential trove of competencies and knowledge gone missing in the economy?

What does the term and practice of "job placement" actually mean in the case of an employment office? In David's case, he has been advised to consult a website operated by the local government providing open positions similar to the US site careerlink.com to which he may apply. In principle, the site represents an extended recruiting agency run by a governmental organization to serve as a collection of all vacancies from recruiting offices without any effective interaction. As the practice is for a labor-office official to have recorded the unemployed individuals in their system and hold regular monthly meetings with their jobseekers, the process assumes that the officials know their skills and abilities.

As there is no direct physical contact between labor-office officials and surrounding organizations, regular meetings between local employers and labor officials to review available talent may introduce a significant hiring opportunity for all parties. The immediate availability of an employee with the required skills to solve a problem provides an opportunity increasingly more important to 21st-century organizational success.

As recovering markets demand the need for speedy response and adaptation, the agility to respond without creating legacy structure that quickly becomes obsolete and inefficient has become the new era of trade. The challenging question for unemployment offices is, "Why does such talent remain unemployed in the face of all this support structure?"

With Switzerland's population of some 8.6 million people, the Swiss unemployment rate stood at 4.63% in June of 2020 (SECO 2020). In consideration of the current unemployment rate and considering the existing effects of the last two waves of the pandemic, that number will surely increase. Switzerland's unemployment rate may not be significant in comparison in relation to other countries', but each unemployed person brings a demand on the social structure of the country. With that in mind, we should be looking for a solution that capitalizes upon the tremendous talent pool in Switzerland—one that could, in fact, reduce—if not totally remedy—unemployment. At the very least, it should be possible to design a process that effectively reduces the delay and impediments to protect individuals who have lost their source of income.

Might a solution be as simple as implementing a national registration system for the unemployed, to be matched against an employment demand requirement?

Switzerland approached the problem as early as 2015 through the project of the Romand (Francophone) and Ticino (Italian part) employment observatory (ORTE), the OAICM[19] (*Outil d'aide à l'identification des compétences et des métiers*"—in English, "Tool to help identify skills and professions").

In a context marked by strong changes in the economic and social environment, ROME ("*Répertoire Opérationnel des Métiers et des Emplois*"—in English, "Operational Directory of Trades and Jobs") was presented as a tool in the service of professional mobility and of matching vacancies and candidates. It was established by "*Pôle Emploi*" teams with the contribution of a large network of partners (companies, branches, and professional unions, AFPA, etc.) and based on a pragmatic approach: inventory of job/trade names, the most common, analysis of activities and skills, grouping of jobs according to a principle of equivalence or proximity. The website "*Pôle Emploi*" provides users with a list of websites used to reference professions. In December 2016, ROME's competency frameworks changed in order to improve cross-functionality when bringing together supply and demand.

---

19 https://www.ricrac.ch/cgi-bin/oaicm.pl

This development consists of:

- reorganize skills based upon know-how and knowledge
- reformulate the wording by simplifying and decontextualizing them

In January 2020, the OAICM was overhauled in order to support employment-service professionals in the identification (or discovery) of new PLASTA occupations and of the new Swiss nomenclature of occupations CH-ISCO-19.

Efforts remain focused upon job titles, functions, and families, common inventorying techniques based upon past structures. Titles become representations of expectation for individuals hired to perform on the basis of expected outcome. The competencies required to execute a solution remain concealed under a general description of the job title and historical function. This method effectively conceals actual talent, increases the risk of non-performance, expense, and probability of shortfall. The missing process is that which categorically identifies specific competencies required to assure success. Simply, title does not equal competency.

An effective methodology must be established to disclose what people/individuals actually "can," "want," and "know how" to do. That challenge is fairly straightforward. If company "A" is calling a position "a potatoe" and company "B" is calling it "a patatoe," our system should be able to recognize the underlying competencies and come up with the same competency package requirement. The marketplace of competencies is set up for a huge challenge, as only the small group of individuals who have categorized the "skills" will be able to identify or match them, and it is not surprising that people do not use them, because competencies are *in individuals* and not *in the position*.

As long as the "recognition of skills and the know-how and knowledge" is not assessed using a common framework, it will be challenging to align with business processes, and align business to business. If Business "A" calls it "potatoe," and Business "B" calls it "patatoe," and Business "A" has only "potatoes," then Business "B" will not want to hire any of Business "A," even if they are the same people. In this case, we would conclude that OAICM would attempt to effect an unattainable alignment.

In order to be an effective employment solution, the employment office should be an extension of recruiting offices, and there should be a regular and effective exchange of communication between recruiting offices and organizations, aligning on common ground with a common vocabulary. It is necessary to produce a common set of definitions for competencies when seeking to fill positions.

Recognizing the importance of the GDPR, if the labor offices would maintain a current national register of generally accepted competencies (generally accepted by industry leaders, educational/vocational institutions, and recruiting offices), while respecting the privacy and anonymity of job seekers, competencies could be attributed to an individual and further associated with a registration number identifying each jobseeker.

The pursuit of excellence in such an endeavor requires a break in reliance on the historical job-descriptive hiring and promotion practices and a move toward the establishment of optimum competency characteristics. The pursuit of a challenging series of projects leading to the demonstration of talent and trail of successes would encourage enterprises to add diverse talent at the optimum timing for the enterprise; in such manner would the resource pool grow to be available to the successful enterprise of tomorrow. Future success will depend on the successful aggregation of talent sufficient to establish and maintain a pool of competent resources—and which are available on a moment's notice—to resolve issues or support aggressive growth opportunities in the enterprise. It is no longer enough to *possess* such talent; current issues require *deployment* of these competent resources.

OVERBURDENED EMPLOYMENT OFFICES FURTHER STRAINED BY THE COVID-19 PANDEMIC

According to a report by the German Prime Minister of Bavaria, the pandemic has caused an increase in both part-time and full-time unemployed people. The employment offices are overwhelmed with this enormous wave of confused and desperate unemployed people. On the one hand, there is a lack of administrative manpower in the offices to handle the volume of unemployed people. Additionally, this support lacks the experience to address either the unique or the general needs of every individual. It seems clear that many staff in the employment offices are also emotionally overwhelmed at the magnitude and diversity of the care required to really assist unemployed individuals. This is further compounded by the skyrocketing number of unemployed. The unemployed turn to unemployment offices—the resource designated as the problem-solver for the unemployed—to support them as they try to meet their responsibilities such as caring for their families. At the same time, the unemployed require both psychological and moral support. There needs to be an efficient recourse for these desperate people. The future of countries' economies hangs in the balance.

Bavaria is certainly not alone. This condition is repeated in employment offices all over the world. This situation is not unique to this pandemic and continues the challenges every time there are periods of economic stress.

Administratively, employment offices follow certain processes, with guidelines derived presumably from past success. Each employee attends to their "AOR" (area of responsibility) with an expected deliverable or result. We assume that every employee of an employment office has a reasonable command of his responsibilities. Is that a proper assumption? This assumption would prove correct if each employee were trained to minimum standards in expected areas of performance. This would extend to delivery of process and guidelines to every new employee by trained and experienced employees—if not also management—in order to perpetuate a successful pattern of behavior.

In the current training model, the unique talents brought to the team by new employees are discouraged and seem to be of less interest than the expectation for the new employee to absorb, understand, and replicate the prevalent, acceptable behavior of the past. The silo is reinforced, and external influence by new employees is minimized by the pattern of training that focuses on specific actions, responses, and behaviors within established guidelines.

Given that each employee is currently hired to execute a specific job, in a specific way, it is probable that newcomers would focus on their specific area of responsibility, exclusive of any talents and competencies held by the new employee. Is that not a correct presumption? Does this not minimize the potential of every new employee? Does it not reduce the potential value and contribution of every employee?

The current model assumes that training has occurred in employment offices, where previously unemployed people were required to acquire fundamental process and guideline skills and have risen to achieve status as fully competent employees. Was there training material to assist in the maturation process? In order to assure replication of desired behavior, this training material should be constantly updated to reflect both past and current experience of the employees. Past experience may be a suitable indicator of future behavior, given similar circumstances.

Once provided, will the training and education enable an employee to understand and carry out the required tasks? Is detailed documentation available to promote further and deeper explanation? Is there a troubleshooting or corrective-action plan to efficiently resolve possible misunderstandings? Does each area of responsibility have a defined level of competency demonstrating an acceptable level of performance? Are there competence profiles to guide performance in each of the task areas/areas of responsibility? Further, do certain tasks require specific competencies unique to particular areas of responsibility?

The obvious requirements of an AOR may not completely disclose the expertise necessary for success. This may surprise, stress, and potentially overwhelm an otherwise-acceptable employee. A given assignment may fail to challenge an otherwise-superior employee, thereby discouraging performance and leading to disappointment and a loss to the enterprise. Each imbalance results in an inefficient use of talent and potential failure of the business process. It generates disappointment in both cases. To avoid this situation, it is necessary for an enterprise to identify potential imbalances and avoid them.

The current pandemic has forced excessive demands on all employees in employment offices, regardless of the respective competence profile and total coping capability. Driven beyond past experience, offices are faced with previously unseen work pressures and volumes and further complicated by changes in the way we all work. This is a perfect example of the scalability of a crisis and subpar results that further delay a return to normal operations.

The model proposed by the authors begins to address the challenges previously noted. By gathering the range of processes and subdividing them into actionable Result Areas, we can break down the processes into individual desirable competencies and thereby construct the ideal employee for every task and challenge—or, effectively, result.

Establishing the Result Areas (RA) enables the identification of process cycles that enable success, because ultimately, it is the results that make a process successful. These RAs establish a basic framework for demonstrating the competencies necessary for achieving a positive result. To achieve this, we break down RAs into individual competencies. These competencies already exist in one fashion or another in the marketplace and may even be known and contributed by present employees.

The concept may be somewhat known in part, but the process of systematically creating a common framework is a significant challenge.

Since we understand elements of the classification, it remains to fully identify, define, and document them within a common framework. Once the body of common competencies is established, the next step is to achieve a particular competency through the acquisition of necessary sub-competencies. To execute this building-block process, we must further classify each into four dimensions (functional, technical, operational, behavioral) and, within these, establish necessary proficiency/development levels. The process described above represents a Competency Framework, a commonly agreed-upon base of competencies or, alternatively, a base of Generally Accepted Competencies.

This framework enables employees to develop and promote their own competence profiles. Each employee may present a unique competency imprint (profile) and structure a desirable pathway corresponding to their preferred career path.

The flexibility allows for experimentation in skills, knowledge, dimensions, and levels of comprehension that encourage employees to expand and discover previously unsought opportunities. For employment offices, this provides a vehicle to systematically receive input directly from hiring enterprises and match the most desirable candidates in the unemployed database. It is an economically efficient solution for the unemployed candidate, the enterprises seeking a solution, and the state striving to optimize its facilitation services.

The matching mechanics required of each RA will require employment offices to understand key components of competency in the search to match talent with task. In some cases, more than a single competency will apply. There will be some training and experience required in the ramp-up to implementation. Nevertheless, a well-structured base of competent potential candidates, introduced over time, will assure a competitive advantage.

An assessment of the number and quality of candidates placed in employment today and the enumeration of impediments to successful placement will quickly demonstrate the value of a systematic matching process. It begins as simply as officials from the employment offices creating a registry of unemployed persons—along with their competencies—derived from applicants' respective documents, such as CVs, work certificates, and school degrees. These unemployed people, in the course of their lifetime, will have almost certainly acquired specific competencies that are not reflected in their CV. This is the opportunity of a lifetime to create a vehicle that revolutionizes and virtually eliminates unemployment. Success begins with the acceptance and support of a Common Competency Framework . . . and this is it.

UNEMPLOYMENT ASSISTANCE FROM THE GIG MARKETPLACE

Referring back to the case of the employment offices in Bavaria, Germany, the program would assess applicants against previously established unemployment-office norms.

Initially, the competency framework does not require a high level of granularity. It is sufficient to have the processes broken down into Result Areas and competencies first and at the same time to plan an expanded granularity of the competency framework for its future improvement and accuracy. With the established first-level competency framework, we can offer all unemployed people (applicants) the chance to undergo a competency self-assessment that will show their potential for integration into an employment office. This would facilitate a number of simultaneous goals:

- The individual would be afforded the opportunity for additional income
- The individual's feeling of self-worth will rise
- The employment office would have a ready pool of additional labor
- A GIG marketplace would be established, where useful work could be bought and sold on an hourly basis
- Governments would maintain the decision-making power to determine whether or not, and how, to subsidize the economics for the unemployed

- Other governmental offices would also be able to use this talent pool on an ad hoc basis

Governments have a philosophical choice on how much to pay for ad hoc labor. They can choose the incentives that they provide in order to encourage or discourage certain behaviors. For instance, they could choose to reward work and require participation in the GIG marketplace in order to obtain part of the unemployment benefit, or they could pay a market rate for the GIG work in order to encourage labor.

Other areas, such as payroll, billing, purchasing, and so on, could be added to the GIG marketplace. These unemployed individuals could be deployed in the Result Areas of the respective employment office as a part-time or a full-time employee, or a temporary worker.

HOW SUCH A GIG MARKETPLACE COULD BE FORMED

The impact to normal government services could be immense. A national GIG marketplace could provide ready and previously assessed competent assistance on a variable basis. Individuals would not need to be purged when they achieved other employment, as they might be more than willing to assist future needs. This pool could be expanded to include any other quantifiable governmental labor-process need with obvious crossover to the business community. But the biggest impact would be to provide government services with a variable, on-demand surge capability to address crises. All governmental processes could be measured for how fast, how accurately, and how effectively they actually function rather than exposed to arbitrary metrics disconnected from the user experience.

Responsiveness to citizen need would increase dramatically, and timely assistance provided closer to the time of impact would result in fewer secondary impacts to people and families, due to fewer missed mortgage payments, evictions, missed meals, etc.

The societal impacts of higher self-esteem for the unemployed, lower mortgage-default rates or evictions, lower spousal or child abuse, and so on, are not easily quantifiable, but they are, nonetheless, very real. The fact is that these can all be reduced through better and more timely service at a cost that governments were already going to incur.

As we have demonstrated, the proposed model provides a competency framework as the connecting element among the area of responsibility (AOR), the tasks to be carried out, and the associated required competencies. To set up a GIG marketplace is rather straightforward and is conceptually as simple as:

- breaking down the unemployment-office processes into Result Areas and competencies
- assessing the unemployed against those competencies

- making an online market where the government is a buyer and the unemployed are the sellers of time using those competencies

The employment offices can create their own internal GIG Marketplace by developing a bolt-on addition to their current internal systems and establishing themselves as the employer and the unemployed as the GIG employee. The employment offices have already defined the competencies needed based on the competency framework of their processes (which the offices have done for their own purposes). The unemployed person would have additional competency-based information taken as part of this existing intake process. Our purpose is not to define the IT transition in detail, but the IT concept is simply this:

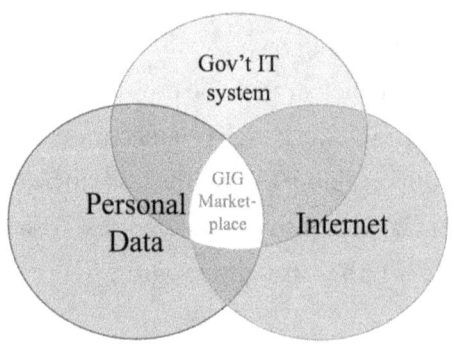

Figure 17: GIG Marketplace

All "willing" unemployed people would be assessed for the needed competencies (or would train and assess to them). With this, the unemployed individual will have the opportunity to discover his own unique current competency inventory and its proficiency level. This gives an immense visibility to the individual of his competency inventory's applicability to the Result Areas of the employment office. Simultaneously, it provides visibility to the employment office of available competencies matching the office's internal processes.

The system would link buyers (the offices) and sellers (the unemployed) in a manner similar to other markets with which we are all familiar.

The employment offices put needed competencies online with an hourly rate assigned. This rate could be less than market, as the person may already be collecting some unemployment benefits.

STEPS TO FORM SUCH A GIG MARKETPLACE:

1. Government competency framework design—Generally Agreed Competencies (GAC)
2. Government designs training-and-assessment platform for competencies
3. Government intake process adjusted
4. Employee profile established
5. Employee reviewed/assessed on competency framework
6. Seller GIG input
7. Employee (unemployed person) acceptance

8. Customer (government) rating of employee
9. Payment to employee (unemployed person)
10. Unemployed people gain new, saleable skills as desired.

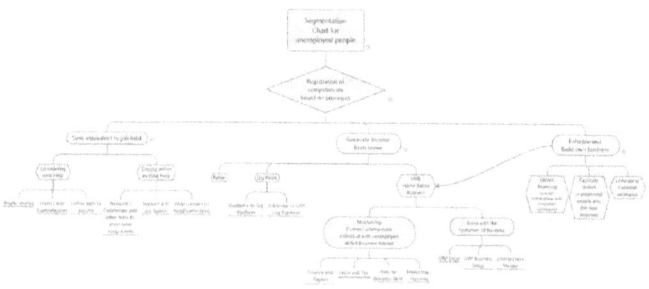

FIGURE 18: Segmentation Chart for Employment Offices

The appropriate GAC details could be gathered with all other profile information as part of the normal intake process. The essential transaction in a GIG marketplace is the "GIG" or short-term work need. This need is listed by the purchaser (the office) with a completion time and a remuneration amount. The seller (unemployed worker) indicates acceptance of the GIG terms, and the buyer reviews the seller's site-level rating (similar to what we are used to). This mutually agreed upon "GIG" is the contract between buyer and seller.

Interested and assessed people could indicate a desire to fill an open GIG, save the GIG opportunity to their personal profile for later review, or ignore it.

The government office would set a remuneration amount, hire a person to assist for a period of time, and then rate their performance within the GIG marketplace. Only performed and rated activities would be paid. To minimize collusion among people, the potential hires could be anonymized, and only their competency assessment and performance rating would appear to the agency. In addition, a remote government location would act as the GIG-marketplace owner, with checks on the system to ensure fairness and impartiality. The appropriate pay could be processed via the normal payroll mechanism, likely with one line item coded so that it is paid for by the statutory employment insurance program, while a second line item is coded so that it is paid for by the local office labor expenses.

There are numerous existing examples of currently functioning GIG marketplaces such as Fiverr and Upwork that could be consulted by a government unemployment office. These marketplaces are a dynamic environment, where short-term services are bought and sold. This is a thriving field, and the unemployment GIG marketplace would set people up to begin to function in this new world.

Appendix II

CEFRL
(Common European Framework of Reference for Language)

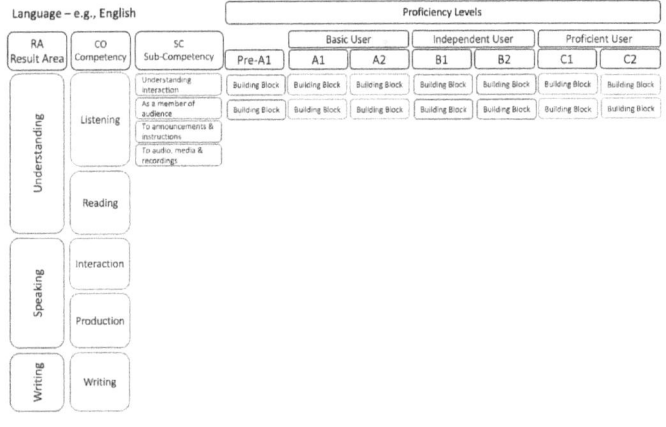

Appendix III

CFR (Common Framework of Reference for the Business Process—O2C

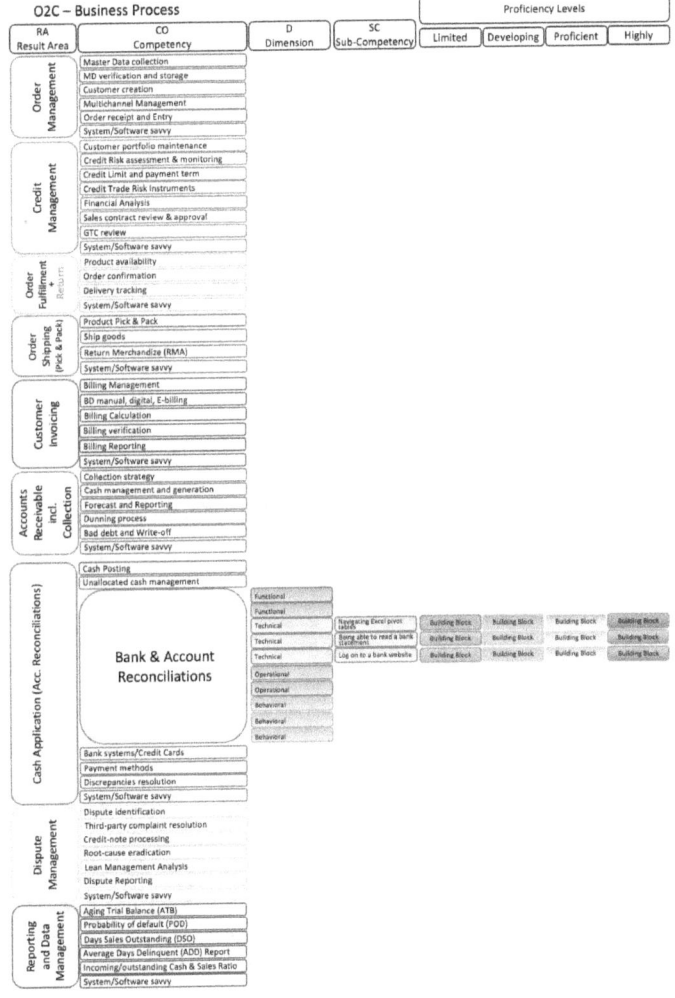

Appendix IV

THE ORDER-TO-CASH (O2C) CYCLE

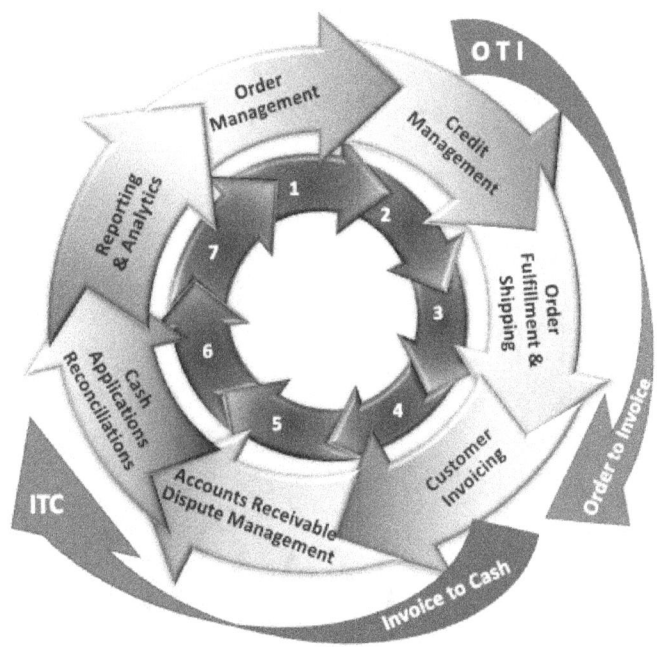

Appendix V

APPLICANT TRACKING SYSTEMS "ATS" (DETAILED)

The key value demonstrated by an "ATS" (applicant tracking system) is as follows. Using an ATS can help save both time and money. Information from applicants is uploaded and organized in a database, making it easily accessible and searchable for human resources professionals. Because the information is collected and organized digitally and automatically, companies do not have to pay for the additional time taken by sorting and filing paper applications. The use of ATS supports respecting governmental institutions and regulations such as EEOC (Equal Employment Opportunity Commission).

Applicant tracking systems allow companies to track where candidates found the job posting—on a job board, directly from a company website, through a referral, or from another source. This can be important information that allows employers to focus their recruiting on the areas where the data shows they have the most success or find the most desirable candidates while reducing or eliminating efforts in areas that show little success.

When applicants apply for a job online, their contact information, experience, educational background, resume, and cover letter are uploaded into the database. The information then can be transferred from one component of the system to another as candidates move through the hiring process.

The system allows company recruiters to review the applications, sends applicants automated messages letting them know their applications have been received, and gives online tests. Hiring managers can schedule interviews and mail rejection letters through the ATS. Finally, human resources personnel can use the same information to put individuals on the payroll once they are hired. These integrated systems streamline the recruiting and application processes for employers.

Some systems also can save time for job applicants. Many employers use systems that allow job applicants to upload their vital information, work histories, education, and references directly from their profiles on websites like LinkedIn or Indeed. While job applicants obviously need to cater different applications to different positions, being able to bypass the tedious process of retyping this information for every application is a valuable time saver.

However beneficial an applicant tracking system can be, there often are drawbacks employers need to consider. Systems are designed to look for specific keywords and types of backgrounds for advertised positions, meaning good candidates who are switching careers might slip through the cracks of the system and not get noticed.

There also can be technical issues. Some systems will eliminate candidates if they can't interpret a scanned resume properly. This can happen if a resume looks slightly different from what the system is programmed to understand or if the resume is more complex than it can interpret.

Using an ATS system shows only that companies/employers are placing/transferring the successful search outside their own responsibility border. They expect a system, like the ATS, to find the right candidate for the right job, and to correctly interpret, categorize, and equally successfully spit out the perfect candidate.

What else are you expecting from an ATS system?

It should provide the right candidate for the right job, when you need it, with the right salary, and in the right time frame. Many employers use applicant tracking systems (ATS), also known as talent management systems, to process job applications and to manage the hiring process. They provide an automated way for companies to manage the entire recruiting process, from receiving applications to hiring employees.

What is the role of a recruiting and hiring agency?

Connecting supply with demand = A supply chain.

The information in the database is used for screening candidates, applicant testing, scheduling interviews, managing the hiring process, checking references, and completing new-hire paperwork.

Glossary

Applicant Tracking System (ATS)   Depository of applicant information so as to better access desirable competencies more efficiently at later date or respond electronically in the event of current or interim interest

Artificial Intelligence (AI)   Artificial intelligence (AI) is intelligence demonstrated by machines, unlike the natural intelligence displayed by humans and animals, which involves consciousness and emotionality.

Building blocks   Business-process source of common basic competencies

Business   Any activity or enterprise entered into for profit

Business Operating Cycle   The sequential flow of repetitive business processes essential to a desirable business outcome

Business Process Management   Responsible for identifying and introducing alternative action toward an optimum solution

CEDEFOP   Organ established in 1975 by the EEC to develop improved vocational and educational training (VET)

CEFRL   Common European Framework of Reference for Languages

Common reference level   Transparent, coherent, and comprehensive basis for assessing language proficiency

Competency   Condition of knowledge and experience wherein individual comparative expertise becomes measurable in four dimensions: skill/subject, sub-skills, level of knowledge, and dimension/depth of comprehension; the ability, desire, and willingness to use a skill to consistent effect

Critical Success Factor   CSFs are key performance elements, indicators of probable success

Deconstruction   Disassembly in order to better understand the components of a skill, knowledge, or experience

Digital Nomads   GIG satisfiers often establish locations that are mobile or foreign, through which to execute the job for which they have been hired, given suitable internet access and accommodation pricing

Dimension   Depth of topic knowledge and experience as compared to the common competency framework

Emotional Quotient   Measures a person's self-confidence, self-awareness, and ability to handle significant stress of emotional experiences. Often tied to potential success in the workplace

Enterprise   Trade entity, institution, or agency in a market

Extended Cash-to-Cash Cycle   EC2C refers to the entirety of the business process, beginning with the portfolio of suppliers and providers, and completed with the receivable payment or payable payment to these stakeholders

Generally Accepted Competency Framework   Common source of business-process expectation and deliverables

Generally Accepted Result Areas (GARA)   At the core of a common competency framework, an agreement of the competencies required for universal acceptance

GIG economy   Source of flexible, temporary, or freelance jobs often involving connecting with customers through online platforms

GIG marketplace   An internal GIG marketplace enables associates to explore a short-term project of interest outside of their usual role. Externally, it provides entities an opportunity to secure key solutions using temporary labor that terminate automatically at the end of the assignment

GIG satisfier   Resources accepting the "GIG" and adequately completing the task assignment

Heuristics   Approach to problem-solving or self-discovery that employs a practical method that is not guaranteed to be optimal, perfect, or rational, but is nevertheless sufficient for reaching an immediate, short-term goal or approximation.

Human Resource   Associates, talent

Job description   Document outlining the characteristics of a particular job for which applicants are sought

Level   Proficiency or degree of adaptation that a specific human resource has demonstrated and is certified to a specific competency

Order-to-cash cycle   That portion of the EC2C Cycle between order acceptance and cash conversion or payment

Invoice-to-cash cycle   That portion of the EC2C Cycle between the invoicing of an order and the cash conversion or payment of the open receivable

Paradigm   Pattern or standard presented to establish a precedent

Procure-to-pay cycle (P2P)   That portion of the EC2C Cycle between the order for goods or services and payment of the open invoice payable

Prospect-to-order   That portion of the EC2C Cycle between identification of a customer prospect and the placement of the first order

Scalability   Scalability is the property of a system or structure to handle a growing amount of work by organically adding resources to the system

Scientific Method   Principles essential for enhancing perspective, improving productivity, and stimulating innovation. Principles include deductive and inductive logic, probability analysis, limitations, ethics, and claims of rationality and truth

Skill   Task based and acquired through satisfactory execution over time

Standard Operating Procedure (SOP)   Standard operating procedure (SOP) refers to a specific set of tightly defined steps compiled by an entity to assist execution of routine operations. The objective of the SOP is to improve efficiency, enhance the quality of output, and improve performance, while reducing miscommunication and failure risk

Sub-competency   Cognizant components that consolidate under certain circumstances to form a specific competency

Supply Chain Management (SCM)   The supply chain is a system of organizations, people, activities, information, and resources established to supply a product or service to a consumer

Talent acquisition and management Attempt to pre-review candidates with a goal to reduce review and selection timeline within the current job-description process

Task A piece of work to be done or undertaken; an element supporting business processes

TRACE, CEDEFOP, UNESCO Organizations researching competency-based business performance

Trolling for talent Broadcast messaging into the job market to secure candidates

Twitch-Agile Condition wherein an enterprise is able to quickly and efficiently perceive and respond to change

Vocational/Educational training Indicates source of knowledge being assessed, trade experience or academic

References

Berger, R. (2020). *The future of the GIG economy.* Roland Berger. https://www.rolandberger.com/en/Point-of-View/The-future-of-the-GIG-economy.html.

Cao, X., Zhang, D., & Huang, L. (2020). The Impact of COVID-19 on Labor Market and Gender Inequality: Evidence from a GIG Economy Platform. *NYU Stern School of Business.* http://dx.doi.org/10.2139/ssrn.3666725.

Duggan, J., Sherman, U., Carbery, R., & McDonnell, A. (2020). Algorithmic management and app-work in the GIG economy: A research agenda for employment relations and HRM. *Human Resource Management Journal, 30*(1), 114–132. https://doi.org/10.1111/1748–8583.12258.

Eurofound (2017). *Non-standard Forms of Employment: Recent Trends and Future Prospects.*

Eurofound, Dublin. http://eurofound.link/ef1746.

Greenwood, B., Burtch, G., & Carnahan, S. (2017). "Unknowns of the GIG economy" *Communications of the ACM*, *60*(7), 27–29. https://dl.acm.org/doi/10.1145/3097349.

Hurley, J. (2018). *Boss determined to deliver the right ingredients for success*. The Times. https://www.thetimes.co.uk/article/boss-determined-to-deliver-the-right-ingredients-for-success-6gtczs8xq.

Katz, L., & Krueger, A. (2019). The rise and nature of alternative work arrangements in the United States, 1995–2015. *ILR Review*, *72*, 382–416. https://doi.org/10.1177/0019793918820008.

McNeill, J. (2019). *Introducing Lyft driver services*. Medium. https://medium.com/@jmaclyft/introducing-lyft-driver-services-ac1ab9488ac6.

Meijerink, J., & Keegan, A. (2019). Conceptualizing human resource management in the GIG economy. *Journal of Managerial Psychology*. https://doi.org/10.1108/JMP-07-2018-0277.

Zhang, Y. (2020). *Will COVID-19 jumpstart the 'GIG economy' in Switzerland?* SWI swissinfo.ch. https://www.swissinfo.ch/eng/will-covid-19-jumpstart-the--GIG-economy--in-switzerland-/45923052.

Sanghi, Seema (2016), *The Handbook of Competency Mapping*. This third edition published in 2016 by SAGE Publication India Pvt Ltd.

Dubois, David D. *Competency-Based Human Resource Management: Discover a New System for Unleashing the Productive Power of Exemplary Performers*, John Murray

https://www.gallup.com/workplace/249332/harm-good-truth-performance-reviews.aspx

Index

Symbols
\"waste\" in our current system 39

A
ability to measure behavioral tendencies 114
academic xiii
agile xi
a more fluent and informative business operation 21
associate, xii
assure competitive advantage 21

B
basic framework for discussion 39
Behavioral dimension of sub-competency 112
blended learning processes 11
bridging gaps xiii
broadcast on the job market 48
broad spectrum of applications 48
Building blocks 19
Business Process Management 17

C
candidate xii
common dictionary of competencies 94
common table of definitions 39
common understanding 28
Competency ix
competency affirmation xii
competency assessment x
Competency-based Business Management 12
competency-based education 11
Competency-based education 9
competency-based employment 12
competency gaps xii
continue learning transformation 146
current employment environment 35
current pandemic disruption 39

D

deconstruct the O2C business cycle 98
deemed immutable 43
deep and diverse talent 51
Developing Proficiency 118
development and retention as a secondary exercise 44
dormant competencies 94
dual enrollment 11

E

educational institutions 38
employer 28
entity knowledge pool 44
e-standardized definitions 96
evaluate and operate on common ground 17

F

facilitates GIG-work selection 137
favoring an assessment of knowledge 151
framework ix
Functional dimension of sub-competency 105
fundamental rethink of the rationale 39

G

General Accepted Result Areas 97
GIG marketplace xiii
GIG solution providers 22
government-run GIG-marketplace 139
granularize its internal needs 138

H

heartbeat processes 97
Highly Proficient 119
hiring system 33
honesty and ethical beliefs 49
human and emotional foundation 38
human resource xii

I

inadequate information 43
inadequate starting point 46
incomplete picture 45
in need of up-skilling 15
internal GIG-marketplace 138

J

job boards 48
job description 45
job titles xiii

L

level of impairment 53
library as a database 21
library of building blocks 21
Limited proficiency 118

M

methodology toward a new construct 39
mimicked behavior 113

N

next-level managers demonstrate 89

O

Operational dimension of sub-competency 110
overcome normal project inertia 20

P

Paradigm ix
preliminary suitability indicator 49
process of ferreting out risky individuals 113
productive utilization 97
proficiency 28
Proficiency levels (Limited, Developing, Proficient, High 19
Proficient 119

Q

qualified and rated ad hoc GIG workers 138
quantum leap xii

R

recognition of specialization 28
resource pool xiii
Result Areas 19
rising GIG economy 22

S

Securing Human Resources 41
self-defeating x
self-directed methodology 9
simplified marketing devices 137
skill, xi
social media 48
standardized xiv
status quo xiv
strategy x
Sub-Competencies 19
suboptimum value chain 43

T

take guidance from the client pool 69
talent pool xiii
talent vetted and hired 44
Technical dimension of sub-competency 108
the Order to Cash Cycle 18
Title Inflation 53
trade 27
trapped by meanings and history in our words 30
twitch-agile ix

U

under- or non-recognized competencies 15

V

vocational xiii

www.ingramcontent.com/pod-product-compliance
Lightning Source LLC
Chambersburg PA
CBHW060826220526
45466CB00003B/988